JOURNEY TOWARD FORGIVENESS:
Finding Your Way Home

BettyClare Moffatt

HERITAGE
IMPRINT

MasterMedia Limited
New York

All rights reserved, including the right of reproduction in
whole or in part in any form.
Published by MasterMedia Limited.

MASTERMEDIA and colophon are trademarks of MasterMedia Limited.

Library of Congress Cataloging-in-Publication Data

Moffatt, BettyClare.

"Journey Toward Forgiveness—Finding Your Way Home"/BettyClare Moffatt

ISBN 1-57101-050-5

Designed by Teresa M. Carboni and Jennifer McNamara
Printed in the United States of America
Production services by Graafiset International, Baldwin, N.Y.

10 9 8 7 6 5 4 3 2 1

CONTENTS
••••

iii

iv

DEDICATION
••••

To my Mother, Helen Thomas Cook,
for all that you have taught me.
I will love you forever.

"Each of us, as we journey through
life, has the opportunity to find and to
give his or her unique gift. Whether
this gift is quiet or small in the eyes of
the world does not matter at all—not
at all; it is through the finding and the
giving that we may come to know the
joy that lies at the center of both the
dark times and the light."

HELEN LUKE

INTRODUCTION
••••

I am an ordinary woman who has lived through extraordinary times. Maybe you are too. I will not give you a resume of my life. It would be too long. You will know me through this book, not by my education, or jobs, or marriages, or children.

I am a storyteller. I believe that I was born a writer, and only had to catch up with my tools of learning to read and to write down my thoughts in order to become aware of what was really happening in my life. I shape my world through words. But not just words on a page. I shape my world with my emotions, and with my spirit as well. I do my best to ask the reader to come into that world of words and share with me the personal yet universal journeys we all take, whether we write the stories of ourselves and others down on paper or not. I collect and share the stories of other people's lives too. As I share mine with them. And you. The most important events of my life were the births of my four sons, and the death of my beloved third son. There were other deaths as well, along the way, and struggles to be reborn again and again. And a continual search for forgiveness, wisdom, joy, and inner peace. Aren't these qualities the ones we all seek?

A wealth of life experiences, that's what we all, both

women and men, offer each other. Some insights, a marked pathway—I have been this way before and you have too. We share, I would imagine, many of the same concerns. Love and loss, aging, satisfying work, recognition, a sense of value and worth, creativity, the joys of friendship, a sense of comfort, the needs of others balanced against the needs of self.

We share a spiritual search as well, I believe. Our yearning for spiritual journey. Our yearning for a way home to wholeness. Our yearning for God. Coupled with the need to practice and use and live the hard-won truths that we have come to in decades of searching. Spiritual application translated into daily life. Can we also share the sense of aliveness and strength that a wise and long and fruitful life, in the midst of decades of change, can bring? I hope so.

Along the way on my journey toward forgiveness, on my way back home in the spiritual sense, that of a deep and abiding connection with the roots of my being and with my Creator as well, along the way to living in harmony between heaven (the spiritual life) and earth (my human journey) I learned a few home truths. I learned to trust my soul. I learned to trust myself. I learned to trust others. I learned to trust God. All part of the journey back home to myself. All part of the life journey that we all face.

My own journey toward forgiveness is an ongoing process that I share with you now, with as much intimacy and honesty, as much soul-searching and soul-laughter too, as I can. My friends will share their stories with you too. As well as some people I interviewed, who started as strangers, and are now a part of my own life and learning, a part of my journey, as I am a part of theirs. Can we share this journey of forgiveness together? Yes.

SEVEN STEPS
TO FORGIVENESS

••••

ONE: RECOGNITION AND ACKNOWLEDGEMENT

We recognize a problem, situation, event, relationship or emotion that alerts us to the need to forgive. We acknowledge the problem, situation, event, relationship or emotion that needs forgiveness.

TWO: DESIRE, DEFINITION, AND DECISION

We desire to forgive. We define the parameters of the problem, situation, event, relationship or emotion. We then make a clear and conscious decision to forgive.

THREE: MEDITATION AND PRAYER

We go within and with prayerful inquiry and an open, receptive mind, we ask for truth, help, and guidance in the forgiveness situation. We ask how best to proceed to heal the problem, situation, event, relationship or emotion requiring forgiveness.

FOUR: INNER AND OUTER ACTION

We act on the guidance we have received in prayer and meditation. We do what needs to be done to clear up the problem, situation, event, relationship, or emotion that requires forgiveness.

FIVE: SURRENDER AND RELEASE

After taking appropriate action in the outer world, we release the entire situation into the hands of our Creator. We ask for the highest good of all concerned. We ask, "Thy will, not mine, be done."

SIX: UNDERSTANDING AND AWARENESS

We look for an increased understanding of the dynamics that led to the problem, situation, event, relationship, or emotion that required our forgiveness. We look for the spiritual lesson. We determine to go forward in forgiveness with increased awareness.

SEVEN: HEALING AND CHANGE

We accept that the situation has now changed. We accept that the lesson has been learned. We choose to look at the situation and the world differently. We welcome healing and change through the process of forgiveness. We allow the energy of healing and change to spill over into other areas of our lives. We are changed. We give thanks.

Part One

How To Forgive

"To be vulnerable and fallible, to have a shadow and a soul, to make our way through life determining who we become by the choices we make, is what we do here. Over and over again, it seems to me, life comes along and says, 'Choose!' The small and large moments of truth that shape what goes into or is left out of a book, find parallels in the small and large moments of truth that go into the choices we make in life about what to add or delete. These are the decisions that shape our lives, which ultimately, are soul journeys."

JEAN SHINODA BOLEN

"It is good to have an end
to journey toward;
but it is the journey
that matters in the end."

URSULA K. LEGUIN

· · · ·

CHAPTER ONE

What Is Forgiveness?

I believe that we shape our lives and we shape ourselves in response to the small and large moments of truth that come into our lives daily and ask us to choose what kind of a person we are becoming, what kind of a life we will have. These moments of truth become our life choices. These moments of truth become our journey. If life is a series of choices, then life is a series of journeys as well. Not a straight line from birth to death, but rather steps forward, from the first faltering steps of childhood, through the leaping and the soaring steps of young adulthood, to the bold and purposeful steps of our maturing years, to the (again) wise and yet sometimes faltering steps of our final years.

We look for both love and direction along the way. There are unexpected turnings, veerings, switchbacks from an original path, a brave journey across uncharted wilderness. There are steps forward and steps toward home and inevitably, missteps and wrong turns along the way.

And there are signposts along the way, as well, if we pay attention through the sometimes bewildering and contradictory directions that the world serves up.

I believe that we are here to learn our own inner directions, our own guidance system, to tune into the best, the highest, the deepest and the most authentic whispers from our heart and soul. To find our own pathway through the maze of outer signposts.

One of the ways that we do this, amazingly, is through the practice of forgiveness.

In a recent spiritual workshop I attended, the teacher spoke of a client who had been stopped in her tracks and had finally, after much anguish, decided to forgive a family member. But still nothing happened. Her problems continued, and she became more and more depressed. "She had forgiven in her mind," the lecturer told us, "But she had not forgiven with her body. Her body still held the imprint of the unforgiven hurt and anger. Her body told the story. She could not go further in her own life journey until she forgave totally. Mind, body, emotions, and spirit."

I was intrigued by this story because I have long believed that forgiving by reciting words or phrases designed to alleviate our own discomfort at an intractable situation, is only the first step on our journey to forgiveness. It is a necessary step, it is an opening step, it is a willing step. But it is only the first of many steps we will take in our journey toward forgiveness.

According to Rumer Godden in *A House With Four Rooms*, "There is an Indian proverb or axiom that says that everyone is a house with four rooms, a physical, a mental, an emotional, and a spiritual. Most of us tend to live in one room most of the time but, unless we go into every room every day, even if only to keep it aired, we are not a complete person."

This book will help you in your journey toward becoming whole. This book will help you in your journey toward finding your way home, that is, finding your own inner strength, inner peace and completeness by using the physical, the mental, the emotional and the spiritual facets of your being in order to forgive, in order to change, in order to grow, in order to make wise and loving life choices along your own unique journey.

Why forgive? We do have a choice, after all, to hold our hurts and nurture them, to hug our resentments, to project our frustrations outward, to recycle our interior garbage through a lifetime of ever-increasing reasons for unhappiness. We have a choice. Yet even when we choose to forgive, do we know how?

Sometimes we do not have the tools. Sometimes we need help along the way, to lighten the load, to cast off outworn attitudes, to jettison the baggage of unresolved pain from the past.

This book will help you, step by step, in your own journey of forgiveness. In my own life, I have found it helpful, indeed imperative, to simplify my journey by identifying and applying seven steps toward forgiveness.

These seven steps are: Recognition and Acknowledgment,

7

Desire, Definition and Decision, Meditation and Prayer, Inner and Outer Action, Surrender and Release, Understanding and Awareness, Healing and Change.

Perhaps your own life has brought you nothing but blue skies, perfect health, abiding love, wealth and joy beyond measure. Perhaps. If so, this book is not for you. For the rest of us, those prayerful spiritual pilgrims who go forward, step by step, into the unknown each day, this book can be a friend, a valued guide, a way through the wilderness.

WHY FORGIVE?

"Forgiveness is the key that unlocks the door of resentment and the handcuffs of hate. It is a power that breaks the chains of bitterness and the shackles of selfishness."

WILLIAM ARTHUR WARD

I once knew a brilliant man with a great deal of potential for making a difference in the world. He was respected in his field, and his family and friends struggled to understand and love him even with all his faults. This man would often boast, "I never forgive and I never forget." This was his mantra, his rallying cry. He could skewer a subordinate with one look. "No one ever gets the better of ME!" he would declaim. He was the unhappiest man I ever knew.

8

Eventually, despite his hard work, his innate intelligence, his own interior struggle with addiction, and the prayers of his family, this man destroyed himself. And left such havoc in his wake, that it was years before his wife and children could come to terms with the impact this man had on their lives. To this day, they are still struggling with forgiveness. His cry, "I never forgive, and I never forget," is only another way of saying, "I WILL not forgive."

We have all known people like this man. We have all, I venture to say, struggled, at some time in our lives, with our own need to forgive. To forgive ourselves, to forgive others, to forgive the past, to forgive the world, to forgive God.

We are told TO forgive. But we are not told HOW to forgive. And many of us, until and unless we are caught in a resentful, sorrowful, or life-altering situation, seldom consider forgiveness. What it is. What it is not. And how it can change our lives.

DEFINITIONS OF FORGIVENESS

FORGIVENESS IS NOT...

True forgiveness rejects:
- Sanctimonious, holier-than-thou pronouncements: "I forgive you because I'm a better person than you are."
- The martyr approach: "I'll forgive you even though I know you'll just keep on hurting me."

- The patronizing approach: "I forgive you because I know you don't know any better."
- The disrespectful-to-self approach: "I'll forgive you even though you treat me badly."
- The no-boundaries approach: "I'll forgive you for anything and everything forever and ever in order to keep your love."
- The fearful approach: "I'll forgive you because if I don't, I'll lose my job, status, security. I'll forgive you because I need your approval or presence. I'll forgive you because I'm afraid of you."
- The brush-off approach: "Yeah, yeah, yeah, I forgive you. So now can we talk about other things?"
- The tit-for-tat approach: "I'll forgive you when and if you forgive me."
- The measurement approach: "I forgave her much more than she forgave me."
- The denial approach: "There's really nothing to forgive. I could never be angry with you."
- The grudging approach: "I'll forgive you if it will bring peace in this household." Akin to children being told to "make nice" and share their toys.
- The conditional approach: "I say I forgive you, but I'm still holding on to my resentments."
- The proud to be an executioner approach: "I never forgive and I never forget."

- The proud to be a victim approach: "I can never forgive or forget what you've done to me."

TRUE FORGIVENESS IS...

- a step-by-step inner and outer change in consciousness.
- practiced in increments, depending on your conscious ability to forgive at the time.
- on-going, depending on the extent of trauma and the intent to resolve.
- four-fold, engaging the Body, Mind, Emotions and Spirit.
- active—a form of energy that changes the person forgiving and sometimes, but not always, changes the situation or person being forgiven.
- expanding, with an intent to forgive one person or situation in your life, which often leads to exploring deeper issues of forgiveness that include self, God, others.
- prayerful, contemplative, meditative, reflective, and devotional.
- healthy. Many physical and emotional and mental problems can be greatly alleviated by the practice of forgiveness.
- loving, both to the person or situation being forgiven and to the self.
- enriching. Energies once bound up in hatred,

11

fear, rage, or guilt can now be released and used for continual growth, happiness, and prosperity.

• wise and creative. Forgiveness is always life-enhancing.

TEN COMMANDMENTS OF FORGIVENESS

from *TO FORGIVE IS DIVINE* by Father DeGrandis

1. Love and forgive one another.
2. Forgive in order to be forgiven.
3. Pray for those who hurt you.
4. Unforgiveness is a type of hate.
5. Make a decision to forgive.
6. Seek healing of the emotions and memories.
7. Close the door to evil.
8. Remember to forgive yourself.
9. Forgiveness is a process.
10. Love your neighbor by being an instrument of healing.

ARE YOU READY TO FORGIVE?

Perhaps you have had lots of practice in forgiveness. Perhaps you have found, throughout a long, satisfying and enriching life, that there are many roads to forgiveness and as many ways to forgive. Perhaps you are able, in an instant, to release resentments and frustrations, to forgive unreservedly, and to move forward, unencumbered by the past. But for most of us, including myself, we learn the hard way. We learn by stumbling, we learn by errors, we learn by mistakes in judgment. We are ruled by our emotions. Through trial and error, we learn why to forgive and how to forgive.

The seven steps to forgiveness are an orderly way to make sense of the forgiveness process. Sometimes understanding and awareness may leap forward before any action is taken. Sometimes change explodes in our lives before we have done more than offer a prayer for forgiveness. Sometimes release is hard-won and action seems impossible. Sometimes our desire to forgive outruns our capacity to forgive.

But by following the seven steps to forgiveness, whenever and wherever we can, we become active participants in the forgiveness process. We become the creators of forgiveness in our own lives. We take charge. We offer up our unloving situations and ask for help and healing. We become a co-creator, with God, for healing and change in our lives. The seven steps to forgiveness are courageous steps. They move us from unresolved rage or bitterness or fear into a more peaceful country. When we practice the seven steps to forgiveness in any area of our lives, we move from divisiveness and war (with others and within ourselves) to resolution and reconciliation.

This is a perilous journey indeed, this journey toward

forgiveness. It requires a commitment to our own integrity and growth, a commitment and a courage that will change our lives. It is not easy. But it is possible. And wherever you are on this journey toward forgiveness, I will say to you that it is also a joyful journey.

No matter how painful your past, no matter how anguished your present circumstances, no matter your age, your gender, your career, your interests, your intelligence, your health, you still have the capacity and the courage to receive, during the very journey itself, a sweetness and a gentleness and a safety that does not require the outer world to notice or approve or keep score. This is an inward journey. This is a safe journey. This is ultimately, a journey of love.

"It is impossible to have a prayer without power. It is impossible to have a thought that is a secret for all energy is heard."

GARY ZUKAV

CHAPTER TWO
••••

Tools For Forgiveness

Forgiveness is a radical step. It requires courage, curiosity, discipline, perseverance, and a healthy ability to look at ourselves, the ones we love, and the world around us in a different way. It also requires energy.

WE ARE ALL ENERGY FIELDS

Magnetic, pulsating, attracting, repelling, both positive and negative in expression, we are all magnetic energy fields of power. This is not just a fanciful expression. My chiropractor talks about the electromagnetic energy of the body, a well-known medical doctor talks about quantum physics (how the universe works), a famous scientist expounds on "field theory" (how we affect the fields of energy around us by our own energy states), a famous author tells us to "sing the body electric."

Begin now to think of your body, mind, emotions, and spirit, all the components that make up the you that interacts with the world, as an energy essence that affects everyone around you. Because of this energy essence called you, you have available, right here and now, all the inner and outer power you can ever use in this lifetime.

Even when you die, your energy essence survives the bodily shell, transformed to a higher level of being, transformed, as many physicists and philosophers now believe, into pure energy. And that pure energy is neither positive nor negative. It just IS. However, the USES of energy can be negative or positive.

How are you using the energy within you and how are you transmitting that energy into the world around you? Chances are, if you're like most of us, your life often reflects chaos and clutter.

What's the answer? It lies, as does everything, within yourself. As you begin to know and express the truth about your essential self, as you begin to tune in to your own wisdom and beauty, your own love and grace, your world will change as you change. As a complete, flowing, yet ever-changing expression of life, created by God for service, love and joy, know right now that you have within you the energy, the ability, the intelligence to take magnificent steps forward into a more harmonious and loving life.

The sooner you begin to see yourself as a valuable flowing energy essence, the sooner you can begin to change the conditions in your life that are no longer right for you. That no longer fit the ever-changing, ever-growing, overflowing you. There are many guideposts along the way. There are physiological, psychological, and spiritual guidelines to help you on your journey of self-discovery and self-realization. It is a journey that only you can choose to take. It is, after all is said and done, a journey toward forgiveness.

CHANGING YOUR PERCEPTIONS

Here's a story I heard again and again when I studied for years in spiritual classes. It's by a well-known early spiritual teacher named Emmet Fox.

"The movies came to the big cities first, and finally arrived in a remote mining camp in the Rockies. The picture was announced and the tent was put up. The residents had never been to a movie before. The tent was packed with cowboys and miners, and at a given moment during the showing of a blood-curdling melodrama the villain began to choke the heroine. An old cowboy in the front row pulled out his gun and fired six shots into the villain. Everybody laughed, because in those days a gunshot didn't mean much. There were only a few bullet holes in the wall, and of course the picture went on as scheduled.

"Why do we laugh at the cowboy? We all laughed, you know. What should he have done? Instead of firing at the screen, he should have turned around and fired into the projector. That would have stopped the picture."

Stop reading for a moment. Close your eyes and visualize the scene of the old cowboy and the movie. How ridiculous to shoot at shadows instead of the projector of the shadows!

Ask yourself: Am I firing at the screen, or am I firing at the projector? This basic shift in awareness can dramatically change the way you approach and solve the problems in your life. Yet how many people do you know who do the same thing constantly, wrestling with the same problems over and over, repeating the same emotional patterns, yet getting nowhere? How many of us still try to solve our problems by firing at the screen instead of the projector?

Please understand that I am not talking here about "Have a nice day," "Put on a happy face," or "Let a smile be your umbrella." I am not talking about mind control or emotional control or any other kind of controlling behavior. I am talking about a basic shift in perception, a different angle of vision, a fresh perspective.

The author of this tale goes on to say, "If you don't like the picture on the screen, change the reel. If you didn't like the picture you were seeing, and would like to see some other, you wouldn't get a cloth and try to rub it off as from a blackboard. You would take out that reel and put in the reel you wanted. The scientific way to approach life, if you do not like the picture you are getting, is to change the reel."

HOW TO CHANGE THE PICTURE

Instead of blaming outer circumstances, situations, events, or other people, we turn the focus of our attention within. We ask and listen to the still, small voice within.

We work from the inside out. We refuse to fire into the screen. We take responsibility for the outer drama we are watching. We ask for help from whatever source we recognize as God in our lives. We ask for guidance and for our highest good, and then, through meditative action, we learn to change our own lives for good.

As action creates reaction, so the universe begins to cooperate with us as we begin to change our thoughts, desires, emotions, and actions to lead us toward our ultimate good. So here we are back to changing our energy. Here we are back to looking within and changing the way we view ourselves and others. Moving past blame, moving past victimhood. Here we are, learning to SEE.

In any spiritual journey, we start with ourselves. Our individual unique journey within. Our journey toward forgiveness.

A friend of mine who is a chiropractor told me that he doesn't work on people's bodies to "fix them" or "improve them." He doesn't serve as a Band-Aid. He is not an aspirin. Instead, he assists the electromagnetic body (his words—here we are back to energy again), to come into its own balance and harmony and efficiency. He asks his clients to look within (to shoot at the projector rather than at the outward picture), to learn to recognize their own patterns of movement, of reaction, of habit, of both self-destructive and self-affirmative behaviors, and then he assists the client to change the skeletal and muscular patterns in the body.

He facilitates change at the structural level.

In each personal journey toward forgiveness, we are seeking the same outcome, that of a serene, healthy, wise, balanced and harmonious inner structure.

This is an ongoing task. In fact, the deeper you go into forgiveness, the more you may feel like an explorer in deep and dark uncharted waters. When I began to interview friends for this book, I often asked them to think for a day or two about forgiveness and to write down any thoughts they might have on the subject. I even gave them a series of questions on forgiveness to prime the pump of their recollections. Their initial reaction was a polite one. "Well, I have nothing to forgive, but I'll search my memory for other people's stories and other people's needs for forgiveness."

By the time we sat down together for the interview, every single person, whether interviewed as an authority or as a storyteller, had reams of life lessons to share with me. One woman told me, "I had no idea I hated so many people. I had no idea I had so much to forgive. I had no idea I had so much to forgive within ME." Each person revealed their own painful steps to forgiveness, sometimes arrived at after many years.

As we then talked about the seven steps to forgiveness mentioned as an integral part of the forgiveness experience, we would often find that several of the seven steps had been taken, often unconsciously, by the person working with the need to forgive and to be forgiven. Then the seven steps

21

could be reviewed in private, and further healing and change could occur. In fact, every discussion, every story, brought further insights to both of us. I was continually learning about forgiveness as I questioned others and applied the principles of forgiveness to every area of my own life.

Yet forgiveness does not happen automatically, especially if we have harbored deep-seated conflicts for a number of years. Sometimes we are too angry or too hurt to forgive at the time an injustice has occurred. Once one of my sons, many years ago, was fired unjustly after several years of devoted work for a prominent woman self-help lecturer in Southern California. Never mind that this woman had also fired, in a space of three months, over a dozen other devoted employees, and was evidently going through some growing pains of her own. My son was hurt, wrathful, and disconsolate. He had discovered that someone he admired and respected had feet of clay. I suggested to him that he forgive her and go on with his life.

"Mama, I can't forgive yet, " he told me. "I'm too angry to forgive." He was wise enough to see that forgiving in the midst of anger would not work, that he needed to clear up his feelings about the situation and then forgive when he was ready to. He could not put "whipped cream over worms," as I refer to the way in which outward sweetness and light often cover up a multitude of unresolved emotions. He did his inner work even as he looked for a job with more potential for him. Within a month my son had a much better job, one that provided a valued mentor for him, taught him wisely, rewarded him richly, and opened doors for him in his chosen field that continue to this day.

But first he had to recognize and acknowledge his real feelings before he could go on to the other steps necessary, including action, that brought him into a much better situation. First he had to change the picture before he could forgive enough to see that the unjust firing was, indeed, a blessing in disguise. It was a great lesson in maturity for him, one that has helped him in his career.

There is a big difference between saying, "I'm sorry" or saying, "That's all right. I forgive you," and practicing genuine forgiveness. It's the difference between a social attitude of politeness, a swift cover-up over feelings, and the opportunity to be authentic with your feelings as you do true and lasting forgiveness work. In genuine forgiveness work, an exchange of energy takes place. This exchange of energy is both given and received. This energy shifts the situation. Sometimes we do not even have to know HOW it is taking place in order to know that it IS taking place. But we will know it. There can be a sense of lightness, a new clarity, a rush forward into new tasks, a sense of closure.

There is another phenomenon that comes into our awareness when we choose to do deep forgiveness work, choose to clear up the tentacles of the past that may have held us, in their unresolved energy, from going forward joyously into our good. I call this the theory of echoes. As we learn to forgive more widely and deeply and thoughtfully than we have ever done before, sometimes echoes from the past come from the subterranean depths and break the surface of our awareness, much as a submerged submarine comes to the surface when it judges that it is safe for it to do so. That's when we sometimes think that we will never be finished with the emotion or the situation or the person who is bringing these echoes to us.

GOING WITHIN

*"God enters by a private door
into every individual."*

RALPH WALDO EMERSON

A feeling of anger or sadness or despair does not mean we have not forgiven. It means we are now forgiving at a deeper level. It means that we are now ready to release even the echoes of the past that haunt us. These echoes are part of our humanness, part of the human condition. We cannot avoid them. but we can forgive them. The more those echoes can be released so that the submarine will not sink into the submerged depths again, the more completely we will know that we have transformed the situation. Our energies and our deep desire for forgiveness of the situation change the situation. This is the seventh step in our healing journey. This is the step when we recognize healing and change.

How do you and I begin to contact our own center of awareness within? There are many ways, some as old as antiquity, some as practical and easy as the everyday things you do for yourself. In fact, there is so much available to the sincere seeker that you can often become overwhelmed in the search itself.

While it is beyond the scope of this book to present anything other than basic workable ways of contacting the inner self and then accepting and listening to that inner self, that inner teacher, still the very search itself is valid. It is as if once you begin honestly to look within, the tools for transformation carry you beyond your original search, carry you to joy, light, understanding, forgiveness, and love.

But many of us are confused and uneasy about the various techniques we may have encountered in books, classes, seminars, or our church home. Do we know how to meditate? Do we know how to pray? What exactly is visualization? I was talking recently to a knowledgeable and sophisticated New York editor. She told me that she had thrown down a magazine in disgust because even in a popular magazine (and she herself worked with words daily in the book and magazine marketplace) she couldn't connect to the author's material about mysticism and meditation. "It was all theory," she complained. "If I couldn't figure it out, if it didn't mean anything to me, if it left me cold, how do you think the everyday reader would feel? Instead of using the tools of meditation to change their lives, they would probably turn away with a yawn and a glazed-over look, because the material was so impenetrable."

Another acquaintance of mine, when she heard that I was going to tackle the inner self and how it relates to forgiveness said only, "Don't give me any Sunday School lessons. I know I'm supposed to love others, love God, do a good job on earth, and care for my family. But nobody ever tells you how. So I'll just stumble along as best I can, because I don't want any preaching. It gives me a headache."

This book is not about theory, academics, theology, Sunday School lessons, or preaching. You do not need an advanced degree in order to find and utilize the tools for forgiveness and inner peace. Here is a simple explanation of basic ways in which you can get in touch with yourself in a more relaxed and peaceful manner.

PRAYER

Prayer has been called the act of men and women talking to God. It can be formal, as in a church, a synagogue, or a temple, or with written words from holy sources. It can simply be our private cry, "God help me!" It can be a treatment for various conditions, as in healing prayer. It can be an invocation, a thanksgiving, a song. It can be intercessory in nature, as when we ask for healing and comfort for others. Prayer, ultimately, is an acknowledgment of God's presence and power in our lives. If we do not feel comfortable with directly praying to God or Jesus Christ, we can use whatever words are comfortable for us, whether we call on a Higher Power, Oneness, the Christ Consciousness, the Light, the Holy Spirit, Angels and Archangels or our personal and protective Guardian Angel.

MEDITATION

Meditation is the art of God connecting with you. It is a listening process. It is a reaching out to know, to comprehend, to accept, to be peaceful. Meditation is never about asking God for anything. It is an accepting, a receiving of the spirit. It is a letting-go of the egoistic, everyday computer-like methods of dealing with the outer world and mundane reality, and instead allowing a true reality, a true perception, to come into your heart and mind. The many different techniques used to reach the meditative process are not the end result. They are only tools to get you to a state of inner calmness and inner receptivity.

As your own limited, finite awareness grows, so will your meditations deepen in joy, understanding, wisdom, and love. Whether you are counting breaths, watching a flower unfold in your mind, contemplating light, repeating holy sounds, or just sitting in the silence, meditation leads you to a deepening awareness Awareness IS infinite. So meditation is communion with the Infinite. Meditation is above all, a listening to the Divine within.

VISUALIZATION

Visualization is the art of creating a picture of your own good in your mind. Sometimes you may also use affirmations (positive words and thoughts to create and keep the picture clear or use denials (a releasing and rejection of negative, limiting thoughts and conditions) to bring about your desired result.

Visualization is more than daydreaming, although every kind of dreaming can help you to stretch your perceptions. Visualization is very focused. It is a way of firming up your intent, creating a picture and bringing it into reality.

Some spiritual teachers tell us that we are always creating our own versions of reality, in one way or another, usually unconsciously. Visualization and its related tools of affirmation (writing out your good, including goal-setting) and denial (identifying and releasing unwanted behavior and character defects), simply put you in control of those conditions that you formerly created unknowingly.

An athlete may envision the perfect serve, as in the inner game of tennis or golf, while the sculptor or painter may translate what is seen only in his mind into a work of art that is seen by thousands. The marathon runner sees himself finishing the race. The child sees himself grown-up. The teacher sees the bright potential within the struggling student.

One of the ways in which I use visualization as a psychological tool in my own work (I am always and forever the guinea pig in any exercises I recommend!) is by preparing myself each day in my work as a writer. Before I begin, I take a few quiet moments to turn within and to see, in my mind's eye, the finished book that I may be only in the process of beginning to write. I see the cover, I see the right words in the right order, I see the finished pages. I see the reader opening the book and connecting with the stories within. I see the reader receiving the material even as I begin to give the material form. This is an interesting way to work, because it connects me with the reader, instead of isolating me with my work. It helps me to know that I am giving forth to others instead of just chasing words around in my own mind.

Everything you think, everything you imagine, is a visualization, a way of projecting a probable future. That is why it is so important to learn to change the pictures we habitually carry in our minds that do not correspond to the reality we want. This is an ongoing process, and includes identifying habitual thought patterns and reactions that do not serve us, and gradually, patiently, without judgment, beginning to clear out and replace those patterns of negativity with more free-flowing harmonious ways of reacting to the world. Practicing visualization, prayer, and meditation can help to create the conditions in the inner self that lead to new conditions in the outer self.

Does all this sound rather more complicated than you have been led to believe? Many people are still skeptical about the practice and value of visualization. And what has all this to do with forgiveness? Wait and see.

As a friend of mine put it when I first introduced her to visualization, "Well, how do you expect me to change anything if it is in my unconscious mind? The very fact that it IS unconscious means I can't access it, can't bring it to consciousness, can't change it." Ah, but yes you can!

GUIDED IMAGERY

Guided Imagery, an offshoot of visualization, helps you to set a scene in order to ask your inner self to bring to you whatever you specifically need to solve a problem, and then allows you to dialogue with the person or situation you have brought to mind. And THAT'S usually about forgiveness.

An interesting example of synchronicity occurred while I was writing this chapter. A professional colleague called me long distance, and in the midst of our conversation, began telling me about the Guided Imagery that she had recently experienced. She had instigated a divorce after many years of an unhappy marriage. At one point, after some years had passed, her ex-husband and the father of her children wrote her a letter forgiving her for leaving him.

This cleared his energy so that he could go forward with his own life. This woman and her ex-husband are amicable but distant. After all, it has been many years since they were married. My friend then related that when her ex-husband fell ill, she was not sure just what to do. Should she contact him? Should she wait for him to contact her? Should she merely pass on her good wishes for his recovery through one of her children? By the time he fell ill, many more years had passed. Their life together was only a distant memory.

"But a curious thing happened," she told me. "In the course of a visit to a psychological counselor for unrelated problems, she suggested Guided Imagery as a way of getting to the root of a problem that had plagued me for some time. I was skeptical, but agreed to try. She instructed me to relax and allow my mind to go to a beautiful place of my own choosing, and to allow whatever person or situation to unfold. At first I saw nothing but dimness and grayness. Then I saw a figure coming toward me out of the mist. To my amazement, it was my ex-husband! He came to me and I asked him what he wanted.

"I want you to forgive ME," he told me very firmly. My mind protested that this was not necessary. It didn't compute. We had no ties between us except for our grown children. He had formally forgiven me for leaving him oh so many light years ago. I felt that I had nothing to forgive him for. But this was what he wanted.

"So I began, haltingly at first, and then with waves of tears coursing down my cheeks, to forgive HIM for all that had passed between us. It was the strangest thing! Yet as I did this internal dialogue of forgiveness with my ex-husband, I felt a great peacefulness descend upon my body and mind and emotions. Slowly the scene faded and I was alone. But something momentous had taken place. Some energy had been released between us. We were both free. I later learned that the illness my ex-husband was suffering from was terminal. I am so glad that his wishes were met. I would never have thought of forgiving him for anything at all. But the Guided Imagery taught me otherwise. Evidently his soul could not rest until everything was cleared up between us, even though I had no conscious awareness of any unresolved conflicts between us.

"By the way, my own problem, the one I had come to the counselor to discuss, just melted away. The act of forgiveness in Guided Imagery showed me how important it is to look beyond the surface of things and to go within and experience a different kind of seeing, a different kind of energy. My ex-husband is dying. But we are both at peace about our years together. Forgiveness has come full circle and is complete between us."

Prayer, Meditation, Visualization, and Guided Imagery are inner tools available to all of us on our forgiveness journey. They include clearing techniques and Inner Child techniques (you do want to be kind to your inner child, don't you?). You may also utilize your own thoughtful and reflective techniques that have worked for you that are beyond the scope of this book.

A crucial ingredient in our journey toward forgiveness is the inner exploration we will encounter in a powerful and complete meditation on the seven steps to forgiveness. This meditation offers a way to access the mental, emotional and spiritual aspects of ourselves that can work together to help us to become whole. That can help us to forgive our selves and others. Then we are indeed looking at the projector (ourselves) instead of firing at the screen.

One of the most powerful yet easiest ways to begin to look within yourself for the answers to your problems is simply to stop and ask, when faced with any number of decisions during the day, "What is the truth of this situation?" This one simple question, if utilized on a consistent basis, can save countless hours of anguish.

Often, when a solution to a situation has eluded me for some time, especially if it has great emotional content for me, I get up very early and walk outside at dawn and ask this question again and again until I arrive at a peaceful answer. It is invariably an answer that is the highest and the best for all concerned in the situation. So awareness techniques can be both simple and practical.

One more thing. Although inner awareness techniques are immensely valuable to learn and practice during our lives, they are only a part of our journey toward forgiveness.

For we are not techniques. We are multidimensional, feeling, yearning, acting and reacting beings. We use what we have in the house of our being, we access what we can, and then we go forward in ever-increasing light and love to right action in the outer world. We strive to balance the inner and the outer. We strive to balance our own needs with the needs of others. As we continue, an alchemy takes place, a true union of the best and the brightest within us combined with the best that we can do and be in the world around us. Always, we keep sight of our original goal, that of true forgiveness.

A wonderful definition of true forgiveness, in all its aspects, appears in Dr. Gerald Jampolsky's book, *Teach Only Love*. In it, he says:

"Forgiveness is the means whereby we experience peace, know ourselves as love, give without sacrifice, join with the essence of others, experience fully this instant, and hear clearly the inner counselings of happiness."

Wouldn't it be wonderful if we could all experience every aspect of forgiveness as exemplified in the words above? Wouldn't it be wonderful if we could live peacefully by experiencing true and total forgiveness?

We can.

The author goes on to say: "Forgiveness is the way to true health and happiness. By not judging, we release the past and let go of our fears of the future. In so doing, we come to see that everyone is our teacher and that every circumstance is an opportunity for growth in happiness, peace, and love."

A MEDITATION ON
THE SEVEN STEPS TO FORGIVENESS

Your meditation or prayer time is, ideally, a private, solitary, daily, disciplined endeavor of both asking and listening. Early morning is best, although some people prefer a solitary time before bed as well. Some people use long walks in order to contemplate and solve their problems. Others seem able to turn within and focus in the midst of chaos, while others can work within a group in a prayerful, energetic, disciplined manner.

Yet, I have found for myself that nothing clears the mind, calms the emotions, balances the body temple, and strengthens the soul as much as a daily private endeavor of meditation and contemplation. Here are some guidelines for the Seven Steps to Forgiveness. You may of course, find your own way to their truth and application.

Sit quietly and privately, with no interruptions or distractions or noise from the outside world. Close your door, turn off the telephone, ask not to be disturbed, do not engage in chatter. This is your time. Begin by taking several deep, slow breaths, inhaling light, exhaling any frustrations or heaviness. Ideally, your hands are held loosely open in your lap, your feet are on the floor, your spine is straight, your eyes are closed, your head is erect. You may prefer to sit cross-legged on the floor or allow soft soothing music to play in the background, or to repeat a word or sacred phrase to yourself, something as simple as God or

One or Om, but that is not necessary unless it leads you to a calmer focus as you turn within.

As you inhale light, envision in your mind that the light is pouring down on you from above the crown of your head, and surrounding you with a soft and gentle clearness. Allow the light to flow down your body and into the earth as well, so that you are grounded in the light. Allow the light to surround your entire body with its peacefulness and safety. You are held within the light and all is well. Continue breathing deeply, as if you are both taking in and breathing out light from every cell of your body. Be still. Nothing moves but your breath.

Now bring into your mind the problem, situation, event, relationship or emotion that you feel you need to forgive. Present it to yourself and to God as a scene, complete with details, as if you were telling a story. You are the detached observer. Here is the scene. Acknowledge the need for forgiveness in this situation.

Speak the words to yourself or aloud. "I desire to forgive. I make a decision to forgive." If emotion wells up within, do not hold it back. Simply breathe through the emotion and continue.

Ask for the truth of the situation in all its aspects. Ask for help and guidance. Ask how to proceed in order to heal the situation needing forgiveness.

Listen. Listen for some clue as to how best to proceed, some word of wisdom or comfort, some easing of the situation. You may receive actual words of comfort, such as "Be at peace about this" or "Let it go." You may receive definite instructions as how to unknot a difficult situation. You may simply receive a sense of comfort or ease concerning the situation. You may find emotion welling up from the depths of your being. You may need to cry. You may feel some physical discomfort. You will need to let go of your logical mind's previous analysis of the situation. You will need to let go of how the answer may come or what the answer should be. You will certainly need to let go of any criticism, resentment, hatred, guilt, or fear that surrounds the situation needing forgiveness.

Beyond the emotion of the situation, there may be clear instructions that require more than a reaction from you, that require, instead, action from you to the person, situation, event, that needs forgiveness. Pledge to follow through on the help and guidance you have received in your meditation. Within the meditation time itself, surrender and release all of your preconceived notions about the situation needing forgiveness.

If it is a long-standing situation, you may very well have to give the situation into the arms of God or the Angels. It may be a situation that requires more than your human mind, your human emotions can handle at one time. So you surrender and release the situation to the highest good of all concerned. You do this in the meditation time itself and you follow through during the days to come, by continuing to release the situation to the highest good of all concerned. Even while you take outer action if so indicated, you continue to release the situation. You continue to ask, "Thy will, not mine, be done."

Within the meditation itself, if it seems wise to your inner guidance to continue with the seven steps, you look for and ask for an increased understanding of everything that led to the situation requiring forgiveness. You look for the spiritual lesson. What have I learned from this? How will my words and actions be different? How can I see things differently? How can my life be changed by these new insights? How can my life be healed?

You then move to acceptance. You accept that your prayer has been answered for the highest good of all concerned. You accept that the healing of the situation has begun and will continue. You accept the real truth of the situation. You welcome the energy of healing and change through the practice of the seven steps of forgiveness. You allow the energy of healing and change to spill over into other areas of your life. You give thanks that this is now so. You are grateful. You continue with your day. You continue to forgive.

It is wise to slowly allow yourself to come back into the everyday world after your time of meditation with a phrase of completion such as "Amen" or "And so it is" or "Thy will be done" or "Thank you, God." Then quietly ease yourself back into the workaday world. It is important to

38

have this quiet time for yourself as a regular practice.

You do not have to have a need for forgiveness in your life in order to use this meditation or any other. You do not need a problem in order to pray or meditate. A disciplined contemplative time for yourself is so valuable and enriching for health and discernment and spiritual development, that once practiced, it will be difficult for you to go back to your accustomed way of reacting to events in the world. Here is a pledge and a promise. If you will practice the seven steps to forgiveness for forty days, your life will be changed in depth.

"Only by being inwardly attentive can we learn to tell what we should take in, who feels safe to be with, where we want to be, what is true for us. Whatever it is we must do to reach the knower of truth in ourselves is our own particular purification."

JEAN SHINODA BOLEN

CHAPTER THREE

Forgiveness And Guilt

To find out more about the role of forgiveness in everyday life, I interviewed Dr. Bea Lovejoy, a prominent psychotherapist in private practice for almost twenty years, who works daily with her clients on love and forgiveness. A charming and articulate woman, she radiates warmth. Her clarity about the issues of love and forgiveness, especially those dealing with guilt, helped me to see that psychotherapy and spirituality go hand in hand, that when we use all the ideas, knowledge, sources, means, and experiences available to us, we can literally change our lives through the process of forgiveness.

"What is the primary block to forgiveness?" I asked her. "Guilt," she answered.

She added, "I believe that unresolved guilt is one of the most common issues in psychotherapy. Everyone who comes to me, whatever their problems, whatever their distress, whatever their coping skills, must first look at their lack of forgiveness. I would go so far as to say that forgiveness is the magic that erases guilt. But first the various forms of guilt must be discovered, uncovered, owned, worked through, and released."

She went on to say that if we look at the two major ways that people approach life—in a fear-based mode or a love-based mode—that the major function of living with love is in living with trust, in ourselves, other people, the world, and especially God. And that the major function of living in fear is that of control, that of controlling ourselves and our emotions, other people, and attempting to control (albeit ineffectively) God as we perceive him to be. A controlling person is a fearful person. Yet that is how we were taught as children. (More on that later!) As we experience more and more forgiveness in our lives, starting with ourselves, we come into a more trusting relationship with our selves, others, and especially God.

I was reminded of a phrase I have often used as a prayer in my own life when things got tough. "When we learn to trust the universe, we will be happy, prosperous and well."

"Exactly! But there is so much to unlearn as adults that often it is only when we are knocked to our knees, when our habitual ways of reacting and acting in the world don't work any longer, that we search for help. And so we go to a therapist or a pastoral counselor, or a support group, or a health professional or some kind of healer, and we ask essentially, to be healed. Then and only then can the process of forgiveness start. And it always starts with ourselves. When people feel unhappy, they tend to operate in fear-based modality. Yet the most freeing kind of forgiveness and the most difficult as well is learning to forgive the self. This is the self that treats us as if we were guilty.

"Forgiveness is at the basis of everything. What lies behind anger and guilt is lack of forgiveness. We are caught in our control trap with lack of forgiveness for the self. People who seem unforgiving experience difficulty in forgiving anyone or anything because THEY have not been forgiven. When we go beyond our ordinary and accustomed ways of looking at forgiveness, we see beyond forgiveness to the essence of a person or situation. True forgiveness, in that sense, erases a wrong as if it had not ever existed. Forgiveness transforms a wrong into a right."

"That sounds really powerful to me."

"Yes, it is. Yet it is easier to explain than to put into practice. It's difficult for people to get to their guilt and their need for forgiveness. Their pasts are clouded with debris. When I do regressive work with my clients, no matter what their problem has been concerning their parents, siblings, etc., there is always an underlying feeling of guilt. This often comes out in sobbing. We have to relearn our deep emotions. It's safe to do this in a therapeutic situation. Everyone at heart really just wants to be loved. My clients will sob 'Mama, Daddy, please just love me!'"

"Can they then experience this kind of healing love even if the person in question has died?"

"Yes. This occurs even if the parents or other family members in question have been dead for years. There can still be a forgiving energy at work in the healing experience. Forgiveness and love, two practically interchangeable words, are still a function of our perception. So it doesn't really matter if the person that the client wants forgiveness or love from or wants to offer forgiveness and love to, is really there or not. What matters is the flowing energy. What matters is the healing energy.

"One of the goals in therapy is to empower people to perceive their original innocence. True forgiveness is based on the principle of original innocence instead of original sin. When we realize our own innocence, we become an original blessing.

"Children have a literal need at the cellular level to feel loved and innocent. Children long to be accepted as they are. It's as vital and healthy to their growth as food is. When the unaware parent holds anything against them, they are unable to feel forgiven. If I know someone holds something against me, it sets up an inner conflict as well as a relational conflict. Then I, as the child, would ask forever 'What's wrong with me? What's wrong with me that they can't forgive me?' As children, we formulate concepts of God based on parental figures. We also set up an internal authority based on parental figures.

"I have found that there is a progression of guilt. There are a standard sets of belief systems that we, as children, embrace and internalize. Then we, as fully autonomous functioning adults, have to unlearn any or all of these messages we incorporated within as children.

"This is not to blame our parents. Usually they did the best they could with their own internalized sets of belief systems. Even when we do blame them, we are taking primary steps in forgiveness, similar to the step of recognizing and acknowledging the problem. Neither of course, is it appropriate to blame ourselves as children for not knowing."

Here is the guilt/belief system that Dr. Lovejoy shared with me:

- Guilt over being, as in guilt for ever being born.
- Guilt over being the way you are—as you are.
- Guilt over being born either male or female.
- Guilt over feeling what you feel.
- Guilt over thinking what you think.
- Guilt over doing what you do.

She explained to me that if you, as a child, do not see your self as forgivable, you will set traps for yourself as an adult. You will set traps for others as well, so that your basic feelings of not being good enough can be confirmed and validated again and again.

But all is not hopeless. One of the functions of forgiveness is to lift the gloom of hopelessness. This is extremely important for depressed people. For those who are depressed, there is guilt and hurt under anger.

There is another common trap that we, as adults, set for

ourselves. That is, we set up prerequisites for happiness. We say, for example, and this is generally on a subconscious level, that we cannot be forgiven until we attain perfection. Some of us say that we can't even be a candidate for forgiveness until we become perfect. This creates an enslaving circle that contains no hope. So we continue searching and seeking and studying ways in which we can learn more, do more, be more. We continue searching for perfection in ourselves and others. We are invariably disappointed. For we are firing at the screen instead of the projector. We are looking outside ourselves for validation. We are looking outside ourselves for forgiveness.

The power of forgiveness lies in its ability to reinstate the value of personhood. The power of forgiveness means that we love ourselves just as we are, right now, warts and all, unhealed, ignorant, naive parts and all, and then, with a searchlight of love and compassion, we set about, sometimes but not always with the help of a trusted counselor, to forgive and forgive and forgive ourselves, seventy times seven if necessary, for all the wrongs we have committed against ourselves in our process of growing up into functioning adulthood.

Forgiveness is action. Forgiveness is an event. Forgiveness can be felt in every part of your body. Forgiveness, once felt, can be known again and again as you begin to trust and love the unique and beautiful self that you really are, the authentic, miraculous true self that you really are. Underneath all that guilt.

"Forgiveness is the answer to the child's dream of a miracle by which what is broken is made whole again, what is soiled is again made clean."

DAG HAMMARSKJOLD

CHAPTER FOUR

Inner Child Work

In our journey toward forgiveness, there are no shortcuts. There is the work of the soul to do as well. And part of the work of the soul has to do with recognizing, acknowledging, paying attention to, loving, and healing the inner child that exists within each of us. This is an integral part of each aware person's life journey. When I first began to notice and work in meditation with my inner child, I wrote the following personal story.

LONELY CHILD, TANTRUM CHILD

Perhaps you know your inner child well. Perhaps, in the course of your forgiveness work, you have contacted the infant, the child, the adolescent within you, and then worked lovingly to convince her that the pain of the past can be resolved, and that old belief systems can be unraveled, and that love from you and from others, awaits her. There are books and seminars and professional help and support groups to help you do just this.

But it's a lonely journey indeed. Just as you think that your dear but often angry, often bewildered inner child

KNOWS, beyond the shadow of a doubt, that you love her and that everything will be all right, an echo from the past comes up to be resolved, and does so by catching your attention in the present.

It has happened to me. We are such complex, complicated creatures, with layers of memory laid down in tiers (and tears), that even if we have had an almost perfect, satisfactory, comfortable and comforting childhood, and are living a mostly satisfying, comfortable and comforting and not too imperfect adulthood, still we have an inner child that needs us. A tantrum child. A lonely child. A child who made decisions from out of the bright eyes of unreason. A child who is not logic, but pure feeling.

And in those multilayered, multidimensional areas of that inner child self, there STILL exists a lonely child, a tantrum child. Who cannot understand deadlines, pressures, stresses, obligations, responsibilities. Who wants only to be held and loved.

Neglect her at your peril. She will make herself known to you. And she will never, never, never listen to reason.

She may make herself known to you through illness, or exhaustion, or depression, or anger, or pain, or any number of rude and unacceptable and unfruitful attitudes. She may come to you in dreams and sit forlornly on the bedspread, wanting to go out and play. She may want ice cream instead of carrot sticks. She may even, in order to get your attention, set up roadblocks, barriers, boulders in the road, all with a devilish smile and a thumb in her mouth. She is first cousin to resistances.

She is saying, "notice me." And so you have to stop whatever you are doing. (She has probably already stopped your task or goal for you.) And you have to pay attention to her.

A recent bump in the road taught me again, how powerful my lonely child, tantrum child really is.

In the course of some much-needed health work, it was suggested to me that I address an issue that my adult self had worried around for months. I was told to write a letter to my inner child.

"But I've already done work like that," I protested. "Several times. Way back when." I went off on my monologue about all the psychological and spiritual work I had done over the years.

Nevertheless. So somewhat grudgingly, I embarked on a three-day writing exercise to help me, once and forever I thought, to recognize, acknowledge, and heal any unresolved issues with my inner child.

The first day, I was to write a letter to my inner child. Actually, my pre-verbal infant, the one who had been ill for nine months as a baby, and had survived, and then had to learn to walk and talk all over again. The one who had been rocked and loved throughout the illness. The one whose parents and doctor had leaned over the crib and said sorrowfully, "I don't think she's going to make it."

Oh. THAT child.

The second day of the writing exercise, I was supposed to go back over the hastily written letter.

"No corrections regarding grammar and spelling and half-formed sentences," were the stern instructions. "Your child doesn't know about those things, she's not an editor. She couldn't care less. Stick to feelings."

I stuck to feelings. If you are intrigued enough to follow along, this is what you do. The second day you add to and cross out and dialogue with your child that you are writing to. Ask her to tell you what the thought is that holds you both in thrall. What feeling, what belief, what conclusion did the inner child come to so long ago, when she could only absorb and observe, but could not express herself? Write it down. Read it over. Ponder.

You may notice places where your inner child might have jumped to conclusions, in her early life, and held erroneous perceptions about the nature of her world, and perhaps come to certain cherished beliefs, in her young mind, about how the world worked. And perhaps now she needs to know that those thoughts and fears and beliefs and perceptions are no longer valid. What IS valid, what IS of value, is she herself alone. And only you can free her of her past.

The third day you ask your inner infant, your inner child, for forgiveness. Forgiveness of anyone and anything and any situation that relates to those conclusions she came to about the past. And you forgive HER too.

51

Then you burn the letter. You tear it into little strips and put it into a glass or metal bowl and let the situation with your inner child be healed, purified, transformed, released by the fire.

Then you listen to her, your unique, precious, inner child. Listen to her for days, if necessary, as you go about your work. She will tell you what she wants you to hear, what she trusts you to hear.

And then you will, I swear you will, if you are conscious and aware, feel a shift within your body, a shift that radiates outward into your world.

It sounds like sort of a "clunk" to me, an "aha" to others. It's a felt thing. And then perceptions shift, and patterns dissolve, and there's a new fresh angle of vision, and life gets easier and the way clears before you.

It doesn't take the place of physical healing, this inner child work. But it's a part of the healing. A valuable and vital part.

It doesn't really matter if you are sophisticated psychologically or an awkward beginner at looking within yourself. Your inner child doesn't care. She only cares about YOU. She'll get your attention any way she can.

What's a letter and three days worth of thinking worth to you? Just do it. Let your lonely child, your tantrum child, be loved by you. Let her forgive you as you forgive her.

And give her some ice cream too, while you're about it.

Part Two

Stories
Of
Forgiveness

"We're all assigned a piece of garden, a corner of the universe that is ours to transform. Our corner of the universe is our own life—our relationships, our homes, our work, our current circumstances—exactly as they are. Every situation we find ourselves in is an opportunity, perfectly planted by the Holy Spirit, to teach love instead of fear."

MARIANNE WILLIAMSON

"We must be willing to get rid of the life we've planned so as to have the life that is waiting for us. The old skin has to be shed before the new will come."

JOSEPH CAMPBELL

CHAPTER FIVE

····

Forgiving The Past

When I first began interviewing people for this book, I thought naively that forgiveness would fit into neat little categories. There would be stories of people who needed to forgive their parents, their siblings, the slings and arrows of childhood. There would be people who needed to forgive their spouses, current or ex, male or female. Of course there would be a chapter on forgiving in the workplace, and hopefully, a discussion of how we can live in the world and forgive what we see happening around us as the world changes in ways that sometimes seem terrifying and out of control. There would be interviews where we discussed at great length the special requirements inherent in forgiving ourselves. There would be chapters in which both I and the person I interviewed would search among our own experiences in order to illustrate and to heal the despair and the rage that comes in situations where we feel that God has abandoned us. Then we must work our way back into a life that embraces and learns from our challenges, a life that leads us to trust God again, on a deeper, wiser level of understanding.

But people and their needs for and their desires for forgiveness do not come wrapped in neat and tidy packages. Thank God for that! It seems to me that we are all whirling kaleidoscopes of intents, desires, conflicts, opinions, you name it, we ARE it! And in the multidimensional, multilayered, many-faceted faces of our being, we find forgiveness of one situation by forgiving another situation.

C.S. Lewis, in his magnificent book *Surprised By Joy*, said that when he looked within himself he found "a zoo of lusts, a bedlam of ambitions, a nursery of fears, a harem of fondled hatred." Wow! Here is an eminent theologian, spiritual writer, and religious lecturer who could admit that within himself lay a confusing, clamorous multitude of emotions and opinions.

So why should you or I think that just by recognizing and acknowledging a need to forgive in ONE area of our lives, that in the rest of our lives we will sit quietly and serenely, untouched by the decision and intent to forgive? I have found that one thing leads to another, just like life, and that when we begin the perilous and passionate process of forgiveness, that it spills over into other areas as well.

When I began to interview Karen, an attractive, conscientious, prayerful woman in her late forties, what started as an exploration of forgiveness toward her ex-husband ended with a realization of the steps to forgiveness she needed to continue the process of healing her relationship with her family, specifically her alcoholic father, who had been dead for almost fourteen years. After talking together for almost

two hours, laughing and crying together, we had the following story to share with the reader.

WHEN THE UNHEALED PAST
SPILLS INTO THE PRESENT

*"The principle of self-cultivation
consists in nothing but trying to look
for the lost heart."*

MENCIUS

"I used to think that I was to blame for everything that
had happened in my life. Talk about forgiveness! I needed
to forgive myself for everything. And I needed to blame
myself for everything too. I was a walking guilt machine! So
if you had asked me then who I most needed to forgive, I
would have said myself. And only myself. Now I realize,
after years of looking at the world in only one fixed way, the
way I was taught, that I am not the only one in these family
and relationship equations. I just ain't the only one! So
while I'm still working through my forgiveness lessons concerning my ex-husband and the way he treated me and my
three sons, I found out in counseling that I had to start with
my family of origin.

"I am the oldest of three children, with a younger sister
and brother. Yes, my Dad was an alcoholic. What else is
new? And my mother, whom I love very much, was just

59

about as co-dependent as anyone ever recognized in an Al-Anon meeting. But I'm not into blame anymore, even though the tears still come easily when I think of my upbringing. I recognize me in them, and when I do, I come closer to the semblance of forgiveness.

"This is mostly old stuff, but it's amazing how it hangs around. I'm beginning to see that I still have things to forgive. Even though I believe that the spiritual journey itself takes care of a great deal of the past, there have been times in my life when I have needed a lot of help from therapy and other counselors. And of course I have my wonderful friends, who help me to see that I am OK just as I am, no matter where I am on my spiritual journey. Because you see, I used to think that I was the only person who felt so bad, and that I must be a terrible person underneath all the acquiescence, because I never felt peaceful.

"As time goes on, of course you have to forgive, hard or not, because the person you are hurting most by not forgiving is yourself. The hardest person to forgive was my Dad. And he's been dead for almost fourteen years! He was a very sick man. He was a very angry man. And my Mother, God bless her, as she lived with this man, developed her own set of dysfunctional behaviors. I want to let these learned dysfunctions go! I see as I grow older how similar I am to her. Hiding my pain. Pleasing others. Never confronting anyone or anything. But I can change me. I can't, of course, change my mother. Although I must admit I have tried to help her, to pass on to her what I have learned over the years in counseling as I confronted my pain. But Mama chooses not to change. That's OK. That's her, not me.

"Oh as I talk to you, I see my past rising up before me, all that family stuff! How can I even begin to tell you about my sister, who is an angry alcoholic, very similar to my Dad, who will not change anything in her life. She would die before she would change her patterns and her way of relating to others in the world. And she probably will die, because of that very angry, dig in your heels and blame the world stubbornness. My brother and I get along OK. Once upon a time we didn't, but we're now looking (some) at the old family patterns. He's married, and has kids, although for a while there he was separated and went through a bad time. But he and his wife are back together now, and they live in another state.

"My mother goes back and forth, staying first with me, and then with my brother. We both feel responsible for her. She took care of HER mother for many years. Now she is old, with a lot of health problems. She wants us to take care of her. We will. We do. But we can't make it all better, can we? My brother and I just do the best we can.

"What has all this got to do with forgiveness? Well, one thing I have learned is how amazing other people are, specifically how amazing their perceptions of the past are. How different their perceptions of events are. Everyone in my family has learned to turn situations around to their advantage. And to someone else's disadvantage.

"My mother used to say, 'In this family, you don't take things that happen with a grain of salt. You take them with a CUP of salt.' I'm seeing how differently my sister, my brother and his wife, and my mother all remember the same events. Everything goes through a private filter. There's a lot of brooding, not much action.

"I led a very sheltered life. Nothing off-color. I went from my family home to my husband's home. I just remember being afraid of my Dad. There was no time out for Karen. I was tense all the time. I didn't learn that I was important. I did everything I was told to do. Immediately. I had no identity. I didn't know I was a person. I didn't know I had a name. This went on for years, throughout my marriage of many years, raising my three sons. I was his and her daughter, his wife, their mother. I was never Karen. I had always been devout, always been active in my church, but even there I didn't feel a sense of belonging, a sense of being seen as a separate person. I didn't feel I had a home anywhere.

"About seven or eight years ago, I found out about me! This was in the spring of 1988. I started divorce proceedings. I started counseling. This changed my life. When you ask me about the steps to forgiveness, I realize that I am still in the very middle of the process. I've taken lots of steps, baby steps, and huge, life-changing steps. But I'm just now addressing the issues of forgiveness from my past.

I would like to change things overnight. I would like to be able to forgive once, take a deliberate action to forgive, and then it would be all over. But I have found that it doesn't work that way for me. It's an ongoing process.

"I guess my marriage just continued the family pattern I was brought up in. I remember when anything happened, anything minor, no big deal, the kids spilling their milk, the screen door slamming, something forgotten, something not done instantly and perfectly, well, it was like the roof had come off the house in anger. My husband could literally raise the roof with his anger. It was like World War III all the time. I felt degraded and screamed at. My children lived in fear. It has taken them seven or eight years too, along with me, to realize that you do not have to live in fear, that there is love in the world, that there is safety in the world, that they are not terrible persons if they don't do everything right.

"I was the peacemaker in the marriage, just as my mother was the peacemaker in her marriage. I tried always to keep the waters smooth. I learned this from my mother. I learned this from being a daughter to an angry, fearful man. I still beat up upon myself when things don't go perfectly. But I'm getting better.

"Yet if you had seen my marriage years ago, it looked perfect on the outside. Traditional southern, big house, two cars in the garage, a successful man in business. But there was something dreadfully wrong.

"I had been raised to be compliant and dutiful. I had been raised for there to be peace at all costs. But I couldn't stand myself. I couldn't stand the marriage. It took me ten years before I knew that something was really wrong, and that all my peace-making efforts weren't doing any good, before I realized that my marriage was killing me. I got to where I couldn't stand myself. I was turning into an alcoholic. Not like my father. I was quiet. I just kept on drinking in the late afternoons and evenings. I wasn't mean. I was just in such pain. I knew things had to change. But the last thing on my mind was forgiveness. Try survival instead."

"How wise of you to recognize that before it took over your life."

"Well, the example of my father was a deterrent to me. I don't know if it was genetics or environment or a combination of both, but when I realized the drinking was controlling me, I decided that I wasn't going to repeat the mess my father had made in all our lives.

"There was a turning point, a day when I couldn't stand either myself or my husband or my marriage, a day when I couldn't go on. I had to get out. I couldn't heal myself WITH him or within this travesty of a marriage. Things were too bad. They had gone on too long. I told him I wanted out. He didn't believe me.

"Well, first we tried marriage counseling. But after just two sessions, my husband exploded and accused the counselor of lots of things, specifically, that the counselor had it in for him, was favoring me, and was encouraging me to get a divorce from him. 'I'm out of here,' yelled my husband. He told the counselor that he was not about to change. There was an angry scene and then it was all over, as far as I was concerned. To this day, my ex-husband is an angry man. And he has not changed one bit! But I have."

"How have you changed as a result of the divorce?"

"I feel like a human being at last. I found out that I have rights as a human being. That I have a brain, that I don't have to live in fear. That I don't have to just endure through life. I know I am a wonderful mother. I see how much happier my children are as a result not only of the divorce, but as a result of the changes within me. I feel a lot better about myself. One son is now grown. The second son is almost grown. In two years my third son will graduate from high school. My life revolves around them. My ex-husband remarried a few years ago, after going with a woman since we first separated. I never had any issues with her. My issues were all with my ex-husband and how I thought he should be as a father and as a man. I still see some control issues here. Sometimes he still hurts my children in thoughtless and demeaning ways. It's hard to forgive that, but they are almost grown now. They are learning to take care of themselves.

"I can now at least grasp a form of forgiveness with my ex-husband. I put an end to what hurt everyone, the marriage, living in fear. I have chosen a different way of living. But my ex-husband hasn't changed at all.

"Sometimes I confuse being nice with forgiveness. I am learning to stand up for myself and my children. Forgiveness doesn't mean caving in and being paralyzed by this man's anger. Forgiveness means I go on with my life and not let the past haunt me. I don't want to spend a lot of energy bad-mouthing my ex-husband. He may never change. He is still the father of my children.

"I have noticed, though, how family patterns tend to repeat themselves. My sister, who is so similar to my father, has a twenty-two-year-old daughter, my niece, who is following in her mother's and my father's footsteps. I used to let their anger and out-of-control behavior hurt me deeply. I used to let EVERYBODY'S anger and behavior hurt me deeply. Now I realize that I do not need to be involved in their lives. I want to break these old family patterns. I cannot be dragged back into that family arena, unless I choose to. But I notice that my mother has a way of involving me in all of that family pattern stuff again. At least I am aware of it now.

"My counselor told me something so important and life-changing for me. It just resonated within me. She told me, 'What you feel is what you feel. Your feelings are not wrong or right. What you feel is what you feel.' This was an astonishing fact for me. Nobody ever told me my feelings were all right. I never learned to share my feelings with anyone. I was shy. It was hard for me to find and make friends. I kept all my feelings inside. I thought I was the only person who felt the way I did. And I thought the way I felt was wrong and that if I could just make my feelings go away, I would be all right instead of all wrong. How could I even begin to practice forgiveness when I wasn't in touch with my real feelings?

"But when I got into Al-Anon, I found out that the feelings I felt were universal feelings. Then I found women friends my own age. They drew me into their circle. Their stories were worse than mine. Their feelings were honest. One woman literally forced her friendship on me. She's my dearest friend now. She was so honest and frank about her divorce and her children and the way she had started over and turned her life around. I knew I needed help. I knew I needed a friend. It's wonderful to have such friends in my life now. They are my family too.

"About forgiving my ex-husband. Well, it's still an ongoing process. But I feel good about one important thing. If I have diverted the path of this family, then I have changed the family patterns, not only for myself, but for my children. I think of this as a Y in the road. The changes I have made, the changes I am still making, change the direction of my children's lives as well. They are living in a more normal atmosphere now. We all have more loving, more caring, more truthful attitudes. And I thank God for that. Because people, especially children, learn by observing other people. You can preach religion again and again, but it doesn't make any difference. It's how you live your life. The outer forms are vastly overrated and the inner journey is vastly underrated.

"There are degrees of forgiveness. And each step in forgiveness leads to new degrees of freedom. I feel much freer today. Life is a journey. That's what I believe. There's a destination. Life is a procession. Until you get there, you don't know that you are there. But I changed the Y in the road. I took a different path."

"Are you easing some of the hurt you have experienced?"

"Sometimes. I see now that I am my own worst enemy. The more I accept myself, the more I forgive myself, the easier it is. I know this in my head, but my head is twelve inches from my heart. Sometimes I don't know this in my heart. I used to feel so guilty! I used guilt for everything. Now I am instilling a new attitude. I don't believe that it is true that time heals all wounds. But I believe that attitudes and beliefs can change and that changes the original hurt."

"What has happened to the original levels of hurt?"

" They're still there. But they are healing. I am healing. Sometimes they still float to the top. My emotions rule my life. But I am a whole lot better year by year. I can see the progress, even though I don't always give myself credit."

"What does your future look like?"

"I'm looking at the ways I can care for myself. I have a

small business on the side, in addition to my regular job. I spend enormous time with my sons and their activities, but that will probably change in a couple of years as they all leave the nest. I'd like to develop my own business. I'd also like to have a man in my life. I'd like to be in a caring relationship. I don't want to spend the rest of my life alone. But I have great women friends. I have great spiritual friendships. I'm now in a church where I feel a sense of belonging. So the best is yet to be. And the forgiveness continues. Day by day it continues."

"Today, see if you can stretch your heart and expand your love so that it touches not only those to whom you can give it so easily, but also to those who need it so much."

DAPHNE ROSE KINGMA

CHAPTER SIX
····

Families And Forgiveness

"It is one of the most beautiful compensa-
tions of life that no man can sincerely try to
help another without helping himself."

RALPH WALDO EMERSON

Forgiveness almost always starts with a family situation and then spills over into other areas of your life. Here is the story of a man whose need to forgive his father made him into the good family man that he is now.

I often ask the people that I interview to answer a set of questions concerning forgiveness. I am always amazed at the individual stories that come forth from the same set of five questions. These are questions we may all ask ourselves, whether we are in the throes of current forgiveness, working through past blame and victimization, or just thoughtfully reviewing the past.

I TREAT MY FAMILY WELL

Philip, the man I interviewed, is an engineering consultant by profession, has been happily married for almost forty years, and has four grown children and nine grandchildren. He is a devout Catholic who lives his faith. Here are the five questions and his replies.

"Who is the person or situation you have most needed to forgive over the years?"

"My father."

"Tell me the story of what happened that necessitated forgiveness on your part."

"There were several things I remember from my youth. The first one that comes to mind was when I was about thirteen years old and my mother and I joined my father in El Paso, Texas, where he had been in the process of re-establishing himself in a new job for about a year. We had been living with my aunt and grandmother (my mother's sister and mother), in Fort Smith, Arkansas.

"My father took us to a Mexican restaurant to celebrate our reunion. I had never eaten Mexican food before. He ordered enchiladas for everyone and they were spicy hot, extremely so. I can still remember how hot my mouth was after taking a few bites of my first Mexican food, especially the outside of my mouth. It burned and stung. It hurt so bad that I could not hold back the tears.

"My father thought it was quite funny. My mother, of course, was very concerned because she experienced a similar reaction. She finally put some butter on my mouth and that gave me some relief. I have never forgotten that experience, and the sound of my father's laughter at my pain, even though I love Mexican food now.

"The second thing that comes to mind is how my father

treated my mother. In those days, he earned very little, but he always had plenty of money in his wallet to spend on himself.

It was my mother who had to work miracles to make ends meet. And she did. My father never took her out anywhere. She always stayed at home and took care of my brother and me.

My father liked the bullfights in Juarez, Mexico, as well as the cock fights staged over there. He liked dominos and poker games at the bars, and of course, he went alone. I filled the role that my father should have played by taking my mother to shopping centers, to the movies, everywhere she wanted to go. I even taught her how to drive a car. For many years I held a resentment against my father for not appreciating my mother as well as for not taking care of her financially as he should have.

"I swore then and there that I would never treat my future wife the way he treated my mother. And I never have.

"Much later my mother had a nervous breakdown and was never the same person again. But in this state of helplessness, strangely enough, my father could relate to her as he did not in their earlier days of married life. He took care of her with such dedication. It was unlike anything I had ever witnessed in their lives together. I began to see my father in a different light."

"What steps did you take to forgive the person or situation involved?"

"Eventually I grew up and could better understand about my father's background—how he was raised and the extreme difficulty that he had growing up and as a younger man. I also understood the times he grew up in. When I put myself in his shoes, I understood him much better."

"Are you still actively involved in forgiving this person or situation?"

"No. I forgave him a long time ago."

"What have you learned as a result of this forgiveness experience?"

"That a person's behavior in one circumstance is no indication of the true character of the person. My father truly loved my mother and she knew it. He just did not express his love in a way I could understand as a child."

"What advice would you like to give others concerning forgiveness?"

"Withholding forgiveness deprives you of seeing the person you have not yet forgiven as they truly are. It's a burden on both parties and limits growth of love between the two people involved. Find a way to forgive. In my case, my faith is my resource of forgiveness."

Not everyone has an abusive childhood. But even in the best of well-meaning families, there is a need for for-giveness. We learn who we are as men and women and how to treat other men and women in our lives by the examples observed in childhood. I have known the man who answered these questions for many years. But only now did I realize that even with a satisfying, well-lived, comfortable family life, he too had to forgive and to come to terms with the important adults in his life. He too had to learn and practice forgiveness.

I had the opportunity to interview the wife of the man who decided just how he would live his life and treat his wife through his forgiveness of his father's background and learned responses. Nancy's answers to the same five questions about family forgiveness produced very different responses. Here is her story.

KITCHEN ARRANGEMENTS

"Each small task of everyday life is part of the total harmony of the universe."

St. Theresa of Lisieux

"I had the most wonderful mother-in-law in the world, and I could never understand all the jokes about mothers-in-law—until I experienced the characteristics of my husband's maiden aunt. She was his godmother and had helped raise him and he loved her dearly. She was innovative and interested in everything in the world. She had served in the Waves in World War II, loved to travel and was frank and open with everyone. She could outwork anyone and took on all the hard jobs in the family, like caring for her invalid

75

mother and later for her widowed brother. But she was inflexible. She couldn't help it, but she could do things only one way—and she knew the best way and insisted on it.

"As a young wife and mother, I was intimidated by her and did not know how to deal with her headstrong manner. It started in the kitchen when I was preparing our family's favorite chicken recipe. She told me that wasn't the way to fix chicken and then took the chicken out of my hands and fixed it her way. She loved to bake cookies, but couldn't find the utensils in my cupboards so she rearranged their contents 'the right way.' It was hard to take her frequent advice on how to relate to my husband and how to raise my children, since she had never married or had any children herself.

"When she helped us move from Texas to Massachusetts, she stayed on for several weeks, working hard waxing floors, scrubbing tile, and (you guessed it!) arranging all the furniture, dishes, linens, laundry supplies, toys and clothes the best way—hers. After lamenting that she didn't know how we were going to make it alone in Boston, she tearfully left and I set about arranging my kitchen the way I preferred.

"It seemed with Myrtle and me that little things just piled up. Nothing was sacred. She wanted to discuss how much we paid for everything, how much we gave in the church offering, what kind of birth control we were practicing, and on and on and on. Many times I lost my temper with her and responded angrily. I knew nothing about conflict resolution then and could only stuff my feelings for so long before they got loose. I was torn between wanting to keep the peace because of my husband's close relationship with his aunt and my own insecurities about my own decisions and preferences. After doing much damage to their relationship, I finally decided to accept her like she was. This was a little easier when I discovered that several other women who had married into the family had worse experiences with her than I did.

"Acceptance was the first step to forgiveness. From her viewpoint I was a young, inexperienced woman who needed lots of help and, motivated by love, she would help me. She had never been in my shoes, but I could try to be in hers. Yet I have found that acceptance can be a trap that sometimes causes me to focus on analyzing the faults of the other person, even while I'm trying to accept them. I also had to accept my contributions to the negative relationship. My unwillingness to enter into conflict gave her the idea that what she was doing was fine with me. By letting little hurts build up, I harmed many relationships in the family.

"As I matured, I learned that forgiveness, like love, is a decision I can make, regardless of another's response. So without really feeling forgiving, I forgave her in my heart. Later I tried to make up to her the conflicts we had experienced that remained unresolved in the past, but she was uncomfortable with this. She would always wave me off, or shrug, or say, 'That's nice!,' when I expressed any positive feelings toward her. I continued though, to focus on her generosity, not on her assertiveness.

"Part of my maturity and growth as a result of this relationship was discovering why she made me so angry, and why my own outbursts only brought remorse, not peace. I realized that I have a right to be angry, but I do not have the right to lash out at others. Also, no one can continually make me miserable unless I allow them to do so. My hurts are not just my own. They affect those around me. When I try to justify myself by making others look bad or wrong, I harm my own integrity as well as the integrity of my so-called 'enemy.'

"The real breakthrough in this continuing battle with my husband's aunt was through the application of a spiritual principle. It's just this. We bind ourselves and others through unforgiveness. We can free ourselves from the baggage of resentment, which harms us much more than it does the one we are angry with. Our forgiveness frees them so that God can work in their lives, and frees us so that an area of our own spirit can be redeemed.

"Any in-law can be a blessing or a curse. I can't get rid of the ones I don't like. I can't ever outgrow my relatives or my resentments like my baby clothes. I must deliberately deal with my hurts and, for me, I can only do that with the grace of God and in his timing. Forgiveness is there for the asking. Ask yourself what to forgive. Ask God how to forgive. Ask others to forgive you. Your own peace of mind is more valuable than any grudge."

*"Kindness is more important than wisdom,
and the recognition of this
is the beginning of wisdom."*

THEODORE ISAAC RUBIN

CHAPTER SEVEN

• • • •

Overcoming The Past And
The Present With Forgiveness

Each interview, each new and old friend who talks to me from the depths of their hearts about forgiveness, each life story I hear, inspires me in my own journey toward forgiveness. Many of the stories start with an incident from childhood or young adulthood and then weave their way onward, with the theme of learning, exploring, experiencing, coming to terms with, overcoming, and always, along the way, forgiveness.

As one friend told me in an earlier conversation, "How can you live a mature life without encountering bumps and bruises, losses and letting-go's, birth and death and everything in between? If you expect everything in your life to be perfectly pleasant from cradle to grave, then you are in for a rude awakening!"

This friend went on to say that while no one welcomes the darker lessons that life often brings us in the course of a long and well-lived life, the challenges, the confrontations, the conflagrations, the painful choices, ultimately lead us to a connection with life that we might have missed along the journey had we had nothing but blue skies and unconditional love. No one wants hard times, but when they come, we are tempered in some way, made more resilient, certainly stronger, hopefully wiser.

I was reminded of these comments when I interviewed Connie S. (I have more than one friend named Connie, so I'll differentiate here), an attractive woman in her late forties or early fifties, who, like most women of her generation, had seen her world change again and again before her very eyes. She is forthright, honest, emphatic. She told me up front that although she had experienced a great deal in her life requiring forgiveness, that the first and last person she determined she had to forgive (and had!) was herself. "Forgiveness starts with the self and ends with the self," she told me. "And there's very little room for self-pity along the way."

She handed me a statement she had written for herself when she had gone through a two-year series of shoulder operations that had kept her in constant pain and cost her job. She had only recently been rehired in another capacity (with a pay cut, no less!)—and was still recovering from the pain and immobility that the surgeries had cost her.

"I had a lot of time to think in the two years when I wondered if I would ever be free of pain, ever be able to support myself again," she told me, "And so I wrote out what I call my Vision Statement for myself. I am not a writer, but it means a great deal to me. I keep it where I can see it, where I can remind myself daily of what is true about me, no matter what the current circumstances are. I want to share it with you." Here it is, exactly as she wrote it

VISION STATEMENT

"Giving is what I do best, and I give to myself in small ways every day. I believe that there are far more rewards from giving than receiving. I rely on the three F's of life; Faith, Family, Friends. Without any one of these, the others seem somewhat insignificant. I believe I need to feel good about myself before anyone else will. I know that life is full of mountains and valleys, and without the valleys I cannot appreciate the mountains. One of the things I know is that although the past is a big part of my life, I can take the good from it and leave the bad behind; I have to crawl before I can walk. I enjoy thinking in a positive mode, because positive thoughts generally bring me bring positive results. I know that we all have choices in our lives and that we live and learn from these choices. I am open, honest, fun, and friendly and will do my best to keep these characteristics. I know that it is far more rewarding for me to be able to extend a helping hand to my fellow man than it is to stand back and point my finger in judgment. I believe in myself and I look forward to each new day."

We then settled in for a long talk and Connie answered my questions on forgiveness in her own inimitable way.

"There are lots of people and situations I have needed

82

to forgive over the years. I guess the person I have most needed to forgive over the past few years is my ex-husband. We were married for twenty-two years. I never realized how bad it was until I got out. It was both mountains and valleys, feast or famine. He was in the construction business. I had to supplement our income while raising our three children by working a variety of night jobs, while taking care of the children during the day. Now they are all grown and I am on my own. It took a while for me to realize how traumatic those years really were. They took a mental and physical toll on me. I was in the hospital five times, each time with bleeding ulcers. This was when I was still married. The bleeding ulcers went away after I got a divorce. I thought all those years that I had to be super mom, super wife, super daughter, friend, worker, etc. I was out to prove something.

"I was raised in a strict Irish-Catholic background, up east, New England. So sheltered. I made a lot of mistakes and paid for them early on in my growing-up. I was married for five years before this second long marriage I'm telling you about. And I had my first child, a son, before I married my first husband. What a story requiring forgiveness and decisions! Requiring adult choices.

"I had a lot of forgiveness to do with my parents too, especially when I was a teenager. I was actually six months pregnant and didn't know it! Only when I was in an automobile accident and was brought to the hospital emergency room and X-rays were taken did the doctor discover that I was six months pregnant. I had to phone my parents and tell them that I was all right from the accident. Later I told my Mom that I was pregnant. This was indescribably sinful to them. Horrifying. I was shipped off to a brother and his wife with six kids in New Jersey. My mother was frantic. She was the one I told. My father never knew. My mother said it would kill him if he knew. I believed her. My mother and the doctor told me that I had to give up my baby as soon as it was born. Those were hard times for me.

"I took care of my brother's six kids and cleaned house while I was pregnant. I hated it. I hated the way I was treated, the noise, the unending work, the lack of privacy, the condemnation. I waited it out. Even when the baby was overdue.

"One day I couldn't stand it anymore. I took off. I walked for over five miles. I came to a motel. I had $8 in my pocket. I checked in, asked the manager if I could stay there. He took one look at my condition and let me stay. I told him that I couldn't go back to that house, I had no place to go. Finally my brother tracked me down. He left an old car for me.

"That night I went to a Catholic home for unwed mothers, checked in there, went upstairs to try to sleep. I went into labor that night. I gave birth to a beautiful baby boy. Mother came down that weekend with a male friend of mine. This was not the baby's father, but a friend of us both.

"When I saw them come in, I told both of them. 'I'm

never going to give my baby up!' I had fallen off the stretcher while being rushed to the hospital. It was such a difficult pregnancy and labor that the doctor said it would be difficult, if not impossible, for me to have any more children. So there was no way I was going to give my little baby boy up. But that was what you did in those days. You gave your baby up for adoption and went on and everyone pretended it never happened. That was not for me.

"Well the friend who came with my mother to see me was like a rescuer for me. He was a good, kind, decent man and he wanted to take care of me. He told me right in the hospital, 'If you want a father for your baby and a husband for you, here I am.'

"I told him, 'Yes.' I knew that was the only way I could keep my baby.

"The home had taken the baby, but I hadn't signed any papers. We had to leave the baby in the home until we were married and then we could go back and officially 'adopt' him. My mother cooked up some cock-and-bull story to please the relatives, because even then, after I had given birth to my son David and had married my friend, no one in the family knew the secret of my illegitimate pregnancy except for my mother and my brother and his wife, the ones I had stayed with during my pregnancy.

" So we went and got my baby boy out of the home and took him. We started married life like brother and sister. We slept in separate rooms for the first two years We were friends. He was in the Navy and we shipped out to Hawaii. We both tried to make the marriage work for several years. Tried to make a go of it. This man couldn't have kids. He was sterile. I found it out only after several years. I forced myself to love him because he was such a good person, but he was really more like a brother to me than a husband. I was so young and naive and sheltered.

"I suffered tremendous guilt. I was made to feel bad and wrong. I was told to keep this shameful secret no matter what. Looking back, I feel great compassion for my young self. I made the best choices I could. I kept my baby against all odds. He is a wonderful, good fine man now. But even he never knew the story of his birth until he was twenty-seven years old. And my father died not ever knowing this family secret. Oh there were always so many secrets back then. People didn't talk about a lot of things. People didn't tell their stories."

"What steps did you take to forgive the entire situation?"

"One thing that really helped me to get this far in my life, was having good friends to talk to and listen and share your views. I tell my friends, 'Don't suppress your story or your feelings. It's important to tell your story and make sense of your life. Bring your secrets out into the open.'

"If my friends judge me for my past, they are not worth having as friends. No one can judge me for my past. I carried anger and guilt inside me for years. No more. My son's real father never even knew I had him. My first husband kept the secret, too. My second husband was very jealous of my first child. Yet it was an unspoken subject in our household. Now I urge my friends to share their stories with each other. There are too many festering secrets in our lives. Things need to be cleared up and acknowledged and forgiven and let go of.

"I agree with you that there are steps in forgiveness. Number one and the most important one, is in forgiving yourself. That is the biggest step. If you can forgive yourself, you can forgive anybody. Don't let yourself be judged by other people's judgments. Just walk away if necessary. I am more discerning now of the people I surround myself with. There has been too much judgment in my life. Now with my friends and colleagues, I look for the underdog and give them moral support. Everybody needs a helping hand. Maturity is one factor that played a part in my understanding and applying these steps for myself. That's the second step. And a third step is faith."

"Tell me about your faith."

"I have a tremendous faith in God in my heart of hearts. It gets me through. When you are at peace with your Maker, you have someone to share the joys and sorrows of life with. My faith sustained me at rock bottom. My faith has deepened over the years. But earlier in my life, for four horrible years, I didn't go to church. I just couldn't. I felt so bad about myself back then. Then a hospital chaplain told me, 'God didn't put you on earth to suffer for one mistake.' I've never forgotten his words. He went on to tell me 'It's people that judge, not God. We are mortal humans doing the best we can at every given moment.' That helped me to forgive myself even more for those young mistakes I made.

"There are several forgiveness tools and techniques I have used over the years. One was my Vision Statement. Another was using affirmative principles. I clip out inspiring thoughts from books and I write them out and put them on my refrigerator and in my journal. So I always have some good words, some wise thoughts to concentrate on. I follow through. I live by my affirmative principles. I would also put laughter at the top of the list of my techniques. I had to learn to laugh at my own shortcomings. You don't have to be perfect. I need to remind myself of that, because I was raised in a rigid, perfectionist household and I still do better with order and structure. That's all right. But I don't have to live up to some idea and ideal of perfection anymore. It's impossible. I'm easier on myself the older I grow. It's an ongoing process. It seems like I never get to the point of being totally at peace, but I am better at peace-finding than I used to be. Better at forgiving and seeing what I've done and where I've come from.

"All you have done makes you who you are. Just you. Not anybody else. Unique. Make the most of what you are now. I expect more of my self than I do of others. But thank God I am not as judgmental as I once was.

"Forgiveness makes life a hell of a lot easier. I am more at peace, more accepting of others. I realize that you won't have any joy of living if you judge others, if you judge yourself."

"What advice would you like to give others concerning forgiveness?"

"Soul search. Look within the self. Say to yourself, 'These are my faults. What can I do to change them? What can I do to forgive them?' Then follow through as best you can. That's another step I have taken, to be honest and objective about my self. If you are willing to get to the core of self, then you can let it all go and forgive the self."

"How did you get through the recent hard times? Specifically the shoulder operations and the loss of your job?"

"It gave me time alone to reflect. In the very midst of pain, agony and fears. And there were always supportive people around me. There were always good shoulders to lean on.

"I asked myself again and again, 'What does it all mean?' I got clearer. As soon as I could, I started giving back to others. I realized lessons of living and lessons of dying. Both are an opportunity for forgiveness.

"Yet I must confess it was so hard when I was ready to go back to work. Even though the doctor did not think I was ready, my finances told me that I was. I had to re-interview at the hospital to get my old job back. I had to interview with my peers. These were people I had hired and trained myself and worked with. And then I didn't get that job, my old job back after all. But there was a lesson in that too. I needed more stamina. I was not ready physically. The doctor was right.

"This has been a valuable time of life for me, these last two years. I came to terms with the operations, with the pain, with the loss of my job. I determined that I could go forward or I could just sit and wallow in my pain. I was determined to master this set of circumstances. Sometimes I am still in pain. I still have physical limitations. At the end of the day, I am like an overwound clock.

"Now I do more for myself and less for others. This is part of my liberation of myself. You earn the right at my age to be kinder to yourself. I wish I had known this years ago. I see with my own case that people tend to take life too seriously. I'm lighter now.

"I'm living more in the now. Yes, it is hard for people to let go of the past or stay out of the future. But I am living day by day as much as I can. I want to be surprised by life every day. I want to get up in the morning and have something to look forward to. I'm more at peace. I have knocked on the door of secrets, and I have opened that door to the light. I have knocked on poverty's door. And I am rich inside. And I'm still here."

"When people have light in themselves, it will shine out from them. Then we get to know each other as we walk together in the darkness, without needing to pass our hands over each other's faces, or to intrude into each other's hearts."

ALBERT SCHWEITZER

CHAPTER EIGHT

••••

Forgiveness And Friendship

For most women, myself included, my friends are treasures in my life. They listen and sustain and comfort and laugh and cry and empathize with me through all the long travails of adulthood. They stimulate, inspire, entertain. They are loving, good and wise. As, I trust, I am to them. Most of all, a good true friend is there. Always and forever. Without measurement. When you need her. When she needs you. And if she can't be there for you, there's always a good reason. And you understand and forgive.

But sometimes, friendships change, just like any other relationship. Friendships, like plants and flowers, thrive on attention and sunshine and space and care. They can be well watered by tears and strengthened by storms. Sometimes. Yet they can also wither and die, or even be uprooted and flung aside in anger. It is a terrible terrible thing to see, this murder of friendship. And it takes a while, a long while, to forgive.

It happened to me.

I originally wrote my thoughts and feelings on the death of friendship for another book, a book I wrote on the soul and the work that it must do in becoming healed and whole. Yet when the story on friendship reached the editor's desk, it was discarded. He had a telling comment when I asked him why. "Because," he said. "You have not yet forgiven your friend. So we can't use the essay."

I realized that his words were true. This sparked a new round of forgiveness meditations on my part so that I could resolve any unhealed resentments still hanging around on the outskirts of that withered friendship. Here is the original story.

MEASURING SHELF LINER

I walk every day in my neighborhood. But I don't go down to the park, and I avoid the large colonial mansion on a corner. That's where my once best friend in all the world has lived for twenty years. She has a yellow country kitchen with brick floors and ruffly, tie-back curtains and an antique-pine hutch and designer cookware. I know. I helped her move into it from a smaller, suburban tract home many years ago.

I remember the day we lined the kitchen shelves. There were thirty-odd shelves, plus the ones under the wood top island in the center of the room. It took us four hours or more, counting the laughter. My friend had bought, not ordinary shelf paper, but the best, most expensive, ridged, translucent plastic liner in the world. This stuff was indestructible! You could cut it, you could scar it, you could dirty it, you could reverse it, and it would all wipe right off and be good as new. So we laid it out on the center island, very precisely, with red pencil marks for the way it should go, and measuring tape, and red kitchen pinking shears which I brandished aloft like a surgeon. And we began to cut and smooth and fit the shelf liner into all those nooks and crannies in that enormous kitchen.

Somewhere along the way, I got careless. My pinking shears slipped, I went off the red lines, and a piece was mutilated, with ragged, jarring, scarred edges, wrong shape, wrong size. It wouldn't fit. "Never mind," I said. "I can fix it." And with a swoop of my trusty shears, I cut the piece in two. The slippery stuff resisted. So then we taped the jagged edges closed and made the pieces fit again, serrated, pinked edges that fit together like a puzzle. The large roll fell off the table and unfurled across the floor, and it was like wrestling a live bear to get it all scooped up and back on the island again. In a fit of laughter, I wrapped the recalcitrant plastic around myself, toga-fashion, and lifting the red pinking shears aloft, I cried, "Look! I'm the Statue of Liberty."

Laugh! I thought we'd die! We pounded our fists on the table, we fell to the floor whooping, we wiped away the tears streaming down our faces. Then we had a picnic, avocado sandwiches and herbal tea, sitting cross-legged on the floor on the indestructible plastic, chuckling, chortling, stuffed with glee. I always remember us laughing. A young, unfettered, joyous laughter.

And this is what happened later. To the friends who called each other sisters. To the one who was short and slender (then) and blond and volatile and passionate, and the one who was dark and plump (then) and sweet and timid and earnest.

This is what happened to us. My son ran away from home. Her daughter moved three blocks away. She helped me take my husband to the hospital. I was there for her daughter's wedding. She shared her beauty secrets. I taught her Kundalini Yoga. I left a difficult, crazy marriage. She stayed with her husband and was cherished. I moved across the country and started over. She stayed in the house with the yellow kitchen. My son died. Her daughter adopted two children. She quit her part-time job. I started a business. She took an art class. I wrote books. She joined the country club. I facilitated death and dying support groups. She joined the Junior Woman's club. I published books. She went on a cruise. I went on *Oprah*. She went to Bermuda. I spoke at international conferences. Her husband prospered. My business did not survive the California depression. She paid off her mortgage. I paid my mother's mortgage.

I came back to our shared home town. She was here still. I encouraged her art and purchased her first professional painting. She encouraged me to lose weight and told me I needed a man. I wanted to share with her my difficult, intense, rewarding journey and what I had learned and experienced. She told me that if I would only think positive, my life would work.

One day it all came to a head. We had both been struggling to find our way back to the place of friendship before our paths had diverged so drastically. I had taken the one less traveled by. She had not moved at all.

We had a talk that turned into a confrontation and then a conflagration. She told me she wanted no anger in her life, that her life was perfect, that I was nothing—Nothing!—but an angry woman. I told her she was a trivial one. Ouch! But that was not all. She told me that for all the years of our friendship, she had counted the cost. She had observed, she had noticed, she had measured. She had kept score. And her conclusion was that I was the taker and she was the giver in the friendship.

I wish I had had a pair of kitchen shears. I would have cut her to ribbons if I had not been so wounded. I would have slashed and cut and scarred anything in my path. But THIS I could not measure. This I could not fit. This I could not fix. Our friendship, jagged, scarred, ruined, slashed in two, was over.

Women give and give and give to one another. Oh we give to other people too. Name a litany of all the people that we know. We give to them. We do not measure. What is sacred about women's friendships is that WE DO NOT MEASURE.

I wish there were a happy ending to this story. I'm twenty

years older and wiser and certainly more scarred than that hopeful woman who measured only shelf paper. I chose freedom. She chose safety. Surely that's not enough to cut a friendship in two. She is the woman I might have been if I had stayed. I am the woman she could have been behind the mask. Could we not judge each other ever again for the choices that we made, and the consequences we bore?

Sometimes, on my walks, I relive those friendship years. And I mourn them. Oh I have other friends. Good women friends. Enough to count on most of the fingers of both hands. So I am blessed. I am not bereft. But friends are valuable. Friends are sacred. They leave a hole in your heart when they are gone.

When I think back to those twenty years, my sister and my friend, what I remember is this: together with you in your yellow kitchen, wrapped in indestructible material, holding the shears aloft. "Look! I'm the Statue of Liberty!"

I remember how we fit the pieces back together. I remember how we trimmed the edges so that everything would fit so beautifully and so precisely. I remember how we smoothed the rough places, and taped the jagged edges, and wiped the corners clean.

But mostly I remember this: We laughed until we cried.

POSTSCRIPT

Writing these words again, telling our shared story, I find new levels of forgiveness within my heart. For no one can take from us those twenty years of good and solid friendship. No one can take those memories from us. So if you were here right now, dear old friend of mine, reading this book, I would say to you, "Will you forgive me?" And I would wait to hear your echo in reply. "Will YOU forgive ME?"

Yes. I will. I do. How about you?

*"This is perhaps the most difficult
of the balancing acts we come to learn:
to trust the pain as well as the light,
to allow the grief
to penetrate as it will while
keeping open to the perfection
of the universe."*

STEPHEN LEVINE

CHAPTER NINE

....

Forgiving The Body

Robin Casarjian, in her marvelous book entitled *Forgiveness: A Bold Choice for a Peaceful Heart*, includes a chapter on Forgiving the Body. I was intrigued by this concept since for myself and my friends, forgiving our bodies as they age, widen, sicken, ache and slow down, and change before our eyes, is a task that all of us face.

I remember writing a book on *Inner Beauty* when I was in my forties. I was also at the time, a runner, a yoga practitioner, a meditation teacher, in good health, and a size eight to ten, depending on whether it was before or after the Christmas holidays. I designed and used meditations that helped myself and the women I taught to look upon themselves as ageless, healthy, radiant, and beautiful. All well and good, all valuable, all designed to help a woman to love and accept herself, including her body, and move forward with increasing self-esteem.

I was never satisfied with my body, and asked incessantly that it cooperate by shedding ten pounds, by stretching taller, by being flatter here and skinnier there. Still, in a youth-obsessed culture, I managed to tolerate, sometimes even enjoy, the body I had inhabited for so many years, a body that served me well in terms of its stamina, strength, and grace. I assumed that with the proper care and feeding, my body would continue as it was into an elegant and healthy old age.

But a series of changes occurred in my life: a bitter, exhausting divorce after eighteen years of marriage, a move across the country, starting over, serious financial problems, a dear son's illness, a mysterious and debilitating illness of my own that attacked both my endocrine system and my immune system, the death of my son and a year later, the death of the man I had been married to, and the birth of my business.

All the learning that entailed, plus an extensive writing, lecturing, and travel schedule for seven years, stretched me to my limits, and contributed to the breakdown of my body. It protected me in the only way that it could. It changed and grew and aged so that I could not recognize myself, the bright, healthy, strong, cheerful, youthful woman gone. And in her place, a middle-aged, heavy, grieving, struggling woman.

I was aghast. I went from doctor to doctor, explored every type of alternative health modality, went through several types of mind/body therapies, started extensive psycho-spiritual counseling with a man and wife counseling team, facilitated grief groups. In short, I did everything. Everything, that is, but love and accept my body exactly as it was.

Years before popular psychological image exercises came in vogue, I had written, in my *Inner Beauty* book, about using mirror techniques to get in touch with, love and accept the body exactly as it was at that moment, and then nurturing and nourishing your body with kindness. Yet when those debilitating changes came, I could not even look at my body full-length in a mirror, without despair. I knew that I was a good and decent person. That I was valuable both within and without. That my worth did not depend on how the world perceived me. I knew all this.

But the body did not. Oh sometimes I would lose a few pounds, start an exercise program, find another type of therapy that moved me closer to healing. I was as kind to my body as I knew how. But it was a sad, exhausting time in my life and it went on for years, until I, caught within the confines of that heavy, obdurate flesh, gave up hope of ever regaining the stamina and lightness and joy that had once been mine so easily.

I would like to write, at this point, that I found the key to health, happiness, and weight-loss by an aha! miracle, by a magic potion, by an affirmation that reversed the years of trauma that my body, mind, emotions, and spirit had endured. What I did find, long after my business collapsed and I returned to my hometown and to a more peaceful way of life, what I did find, oh hard-won, painful wisdom!—was that the only way I could continue to live in my body on this planet with any degree of grace and contentment, was to honor my body exactly as it was now, ten traumatic years later. And to look for the spiritual lessons that my body had taught me.

Here are some of the lessons. I believe that if I had not encountered illness and a great change in my body, that I would never have understood the illness and debilitating changes that my son with AIDS encountered in his own journey. I would never have had the will and the opportunity to enter into the years of working in the AIDS crisis, with mothers, fathers, brothers, sisters, lovers, spouses, friends. I would never have known how it feels for hearts to break open and bodies to fail their owners, never known of the compassion, unconditional love, and caring of the thousands of people I met who shared their life stories, their luminous courage, and their pain with me.

My body expanded to meet the challenges that it encountered. My body mothered both me and the people I met as best it could. I write this from the depths of my heart, knowing full well that I do not have all the answers as to why someone falls ill, why someone dies, why the body betrays its owner, even while the soul flies forward into a final peace. Each person I met in those tumultuous, war-torn years was struggling with the deepest questions of life and death. They were struggling, above all, with forgiveness. As was I.

I write this book because I am still learning forgiveness. Not just of my body, but of all those traumas of all those years. I wish that I could report to you that by looking into the mirror the pounds would magically fall off, and the years would disappear. But those years are written on the body.

What I do now is follow the seven steps of forgiveness in regard to my body. I recognize and I acknowledge, I desire and define and decide, I meditate and pray, I take both inner and outer action, I surrender and release, I continue with understanding and awareness, and I ask for healing and change. Slowly my body responds, as it takes its own tentative steps into believing that I love and accept it. Slowly it lightens within. It grows stronger. Old illnesses have been reversed. Fatigue is no longer a constant companion.

Yet there is another component to this story of forgiving the body. There is another answer. There is another insight. There is, above all, another spiritual lesson for me to learn. In the still, small hours of the morning, when prayer and meditation have a chance of breaking through the barriers of the everyday world and the conscious mind, and the still, small voice of the self whispers its truths so that we can transform even our most traumatic lessons into grace, these words came to me. "You no longer need to use your body as a trauma center."

In a rush of realization, the words echoed through me.

"You no longer need to use your body as a trauma center."

From that moment on, the old lessons, the old insights, fell away, and I went a step further in my journey. Although I was, at the time, again engaged in a journey of caregiving for another dear family member, a long and exhausting journey that seemed to have no end (a subject for another chapter), the words that had echoed through me served as a mantra for me as I went about my daily tasks.

Slowly I learned that I did not have to take on the cares of the world in order to serve. Slowly I learned that I did not have to take on and absorb other people's pain. Slowly I learned that loving myself while I loved others did not require the processing of other people's anger, shame, grief, guilt, fear, and physical trauma. Slowly I learned to step back a little (even as I went forward in understanding, ah paradox!), step back and breathe deeply, gain perspective, instead of always rushing forward to alleviate another person's distress. It is a journey that continues for me to this day.

I am ten years older than when I first started this journey toward forgiveness. I have learned the lessons my body had to teach me, in order that I could love, accept and serve others. And whatever its shape, size, or condition, I know now that I am not my body, although I have a body. I am not my mind, although I have a mind. I am not my emotions, although I ride my emotions both in my personal and my writing life, as a captain rides the tiller of a boat that carries its owner on the tides and the swells of the sea. The spirit within is what carries me. The soul within is what sustains me. I continue to forgive my body, even as I continue to love all that it has taught me in this tumultuous journey to the very heart of self.

"One of my colleagues in the field of caregiving once said, 'There are only four kinds of people in this world:

- *Those who have been caregivers;*
- *Those who currently are caregivers;*
- *Those who will be caregivers;*
- *Those who will need caregivers.'*
That pretty much covers all of us!"

ROSALYNN CARTER

CHAPTER TEN

••••

Forgiveness And Caregiving

Nowhere is forgiveness more misunderstood than in caring for a person who is ill and dying. Nowhere is heroism, self-sacrifice, and the practice of unconditional love more misused. Somehow we expect, as do our loved ones who have need of us, that the road to caregiving will lead us to a deeper understanding of both life and death, a deeper expression of love and solicitude. It will. It does. It also leads us to exhaustion, resentment, sometimes bitterness, and the opening up within us of every unhealed emotion we have ever held. I know. Words like rage, shame, grief, guilt, and fear take on intense emotional resonance when you are in the midst of caregiving. I have been there more than once.

Caregiving is both a purifying process and a deep part of our spiritual journey. And it is difficult. It can kill us along the way if we are not aware. Our own expectations of ourselves can never match the heroic and superhuman powers we are expected to possess and exercise on behalf of others, even as we go through our own dark nights of the soul.

My own experiences with caregiving started with the illness of my father. I was nineteen, with two babies in diapers, a husband who was overseas, two younger sisters in school, a mother who worked at her first job. When my father became too ill to be cared for at home, he would go to the veterans' hospital, only to come home to the back bedroom, where he suffered from constant nightmares that reverberated through the tiny tract home in which we all lived. I was very close to my father, and we grew even closer during the early stages of his illness, but I was young, emotional, and overworked, and by the end of his life, was conscious only of a vast relief coupled with a great emptiness.

This was only the first of many opportunities to teach me about life in the midst of death. I struggled greatly when the man I had been married to for eighteen years, and divorced from for three, suffered from both mental and physical illness and died without forgiving me for leaving him.

But I was, by that time, fully engaged in the work of caring for my beloved son Michael through his journey through AIDS. His legacy of love, the luminosity and sweetness of this dear young man who taught all his family lasting lessons of unconditional love and forgiveness, changed my life.

For years I worked to do the work I felt that he would have done, had he lived. It was a valuable, intense time for me. And I regret nothing of those seven years except that I would now, looking back from a more balanced perspective, have been kinder to myself. I would have found time for joy and healing and balance during this intense journey of the spirit.

As I write these words, I have been engaged in my mother's three-year struggle with a debilitating and terminal illness. I am more tired than I have ever been. The end is not yet in sight. And I ponder the lessons I am still learning about caregiving and forgiveness.

This time, I am learning, as I mentioned earlier, that my body is no longer required to serve as a trauma center for others. It is no longer to serve as a shock absorber for the painful illnesses of others. No longer a repository for their anguished emotions. I can love and I can serve. And I still do.

But finally, slowly, painfully, bit by bit, I am coming to learn the lessons of caregiving. That I am a human being, not a superhuman savior, that I am engaged in my own journey of emotional and spiritual understanding and that yes, my emotions DO matter, even in the midst of my loved one's terrible, insatiable, anguished needs.

And I must forgive myself for not being able to meet those needs. I must forgive myself. Perhaps you too are involved in a loved one's journey toward death. Perhaps you love them with all your heart. And yet you may very well find, it is, in fact, a certainty that you will find, that you are not able to do all and be all that you had hoped for when you began this exhausting and perilous journey. There are times when you can go no further. And there are times when you too must grieve. Grieve in the midst of the caring and the caregiving.

At the beginning of my mother's three-year battle with illness, I wrote a personal essay about my feelings.

I was only beginning to come to terms with the knowledge that my mother was changing from the strong, cheerful, busy independent woman she had always been, and that our roles were not only reversed, a common phenomenon when daughters care for their parents, but that I had lost my mother. Here is the essay.

FOLDING SHEETS

My mother calls me on the phone, complaining. She wants me to come over and help her fold her sheets. The laundry has tired her. I go, of course. We fold the sheets together, to her command, inserting corners just so, stacking and pressing the creases.

When I see my mother these days, and I see her almost every day, I am struck with a wave of emotions—pity, terror, exasperation, tenderness, coupled with a yearning, unfathomable love. She is a small bird now, in protective custody, where once she was a chirping, enthusiastic, busy, bustling sparrow.

"I miss my mother," she says to me as we fold the sheets. "I call out to her at night, and almost think I can see her form, vanishing down the hall. I miss my mother," she says again, and starts to cry.

Her mother died on her 79th birthday, smiling in her

rocker, with the sun shining across her face. My mother discovered her mother just like this, when my mother came home from work. I remember that day.

Ten years ago, my mother held me as I cried into her arms that I was leaving my husband. Nine years ago my grandson died. We came to mother's house from all across the country to lay him to rest. Eight years ago, my mother sent me off across the country to a new life, without recriminations. Seven years ago, my mother held me as my son lay dying. Six years ago, my mother came across the country to take care of her great-grandchildren. Five years ago, my mother sorted her memories of thirty years, as I helped her leave the house next to the house where her own mother had died, and moved her into a condo. Four years ago, my mother made the trek again to California, where she helped me move into new offices and living quarters. Three years ago, my mother staged a weekend family reunion and 75th birthday party for herself out in the countryside. She worked for weeks on this party. Sixty family members came to help her celebrate. Two years ago, my mother helped me move back from California and into a house near her. I was starting over. Again. I needed her. Now it is one year later. Now my mother has been diagnosed with a lingering, chronic, debilitating disease.

My mother cries for her mother. She is very close to the age when her own mother died.

What will I do? Oh I know what I will do NOW. I will

fold sheets and get up on step-stools to hunt for casseroles, and take her to the doctor, and clean her house, and bring food, and take her for outings. I will undo the zipper in the back of her church dress that she cannot reach, and kneel in front of her to guide her shoes onto her tiny feet. I will listen to her, and slow my steps to her faltering ones, and watch her as she dozes. But what will I do THEN?

My sons are scattered all over the country. They have busy, important lives. They will not come to help me fold MY sheets. Sons don't do that. Who will mother ME? Who will help me when I cry out again, and again, and yet again, at the loss of the one person left in the world who loves me just as I am, without conditions, yet with great, unreachable expectations, and for all time and eternity? Who will love me forever, just as her own mother loved her? Who will comfort me?

I miss my mother.

As I write this book, I have no way of knowing whether my mother will still be alive for me to read it to her. Her mental faculties are going, even as her body stiffens and wastes away. She has become a frightened and confused child, so tiny, so weak, so needy, that it takes all my courage and all my love to be with her daily. And yet the love IS there. "I will love you forever, Mama," I whisper to her as I kiss her good-bye.

And then I get into my car and drive away from the

nursing home, and ask for forgiveness. Why do I ask for forgiveness? Aren't I doing all that a daughter can do? All that anyone can do? I ask for forgiveness because the human being that I am wants release for her and for me. I ask for forgiveness because I question the wisdom of her continuing to live in so damaged a body and mind. I ask for forgiveness because I do not know God's will for all of us (my sisters, my mother and myself) in this terrible and exhausting time, and I struggle to understand these final and irrevocable lessons of holding on and letting go, of loving dearly and releasing the outcome.

Sometimes forgiveness is named by other words and attitudes than those customary. Sometimes it is called love. Sometimes, it seems to me, it is called endurance. Sometimes it is called surrender.

Once I interviewed Marianne Williamson, the well-known woman spiritual teacher of A Course In Miracles, for an earlier book I wrote on death and dying, called *Gifts For The Living*. In the interview, she told me and the readers that when someone is ill, when someone is dying, this is what you do:

"And when you feel like 'What can I do?' just know that your showing up and holding love in your mind means you are bringing the power of God. You are affecting the forces of comfort on an invisible level. God will do his part if you'll do yours. If you will just show up. He will tell you what to say, what to do, perhaps just sit there. You will be transformed through an attitude of service. Just don't run away. The only enemy is your tendency to want to shut down and run away. The only thing to fear is the fear itself. Just stand forth and ask God continually: 'Open my heart and we'll do everything right.'"

I remembered Marianne's words, spoken to me originally as we both worked within the AIDS crisis, again when my mother first became ill. I remember her words now, years later, as I aim my car along its daily route, a route I could now take with my eyes closed if need be, because it is so familiar to me, so well-worn. The drive to my mother's last and smallest place. I wonder each day if she will be lucid and loving, or lost in the terrible hallucinations that bewilder and terrify her.

"Just show up." The words echo in my mind. Just be there for them. Be the witness. Be the helping hand. Be the loving heart. Just show up.

I show up. Daily I show up. I hold my mother's hand. I struggle to understand the lessons of her life and the love she has taught me. I struggle to forgive. And I still miss my mother.

FORGIVING THE SYSTEM

I asked a dear friend of mine, who has not only written books in the caregiving field, but who also went through her own long and terrible caregiving ordeal with her parents, to tell me of her experiences as a caregiver. In fact, her father died of a stroke taking care of her mother, who had Alzheimer's disease for many years, and finally and mercifully died about two years ago.

My friend learned first-hand what it was to find care for someone whose mental faculties were gone, but whose body needed care over a period of several years. I asked her to write out her thoughts on the subject of forgiveness and when she began, she found that now, long after the fact, her anger had centered on the system that thwarted her every attempt to get help for her parents, even while she had to continue to work as a full-time writer in order to support herself and to help them.

"The most animosity I ever felt was against an institution, rather than a person. So that's what I will write about to answer your questions about forgiveness.

"The Riverside Department of Public Social Services (when I went to get my parents on Medi-Cal, California's version of Medicaid, after their Medicare benefits ran out), was one of the most frustrating experiences I've ever had. My parents had been declared incompetent to look after themselves or to make their own decisions.

"The DPSS staff were cold, authoritarian, unhelpful, rigid, and in more than one instance, lied. The case worker in charge told me that when I called in with information to ask for her by number, not by her name. Can you believe that! I had to fight for months to get help for my parents. My father died of a stroke during this interminable process.

"As I continued as advocate for my remaining parent's long-term care needs, my anger coalesced against the system. As I mulled over all that had happened and had not happened, the situation itself became, first the focus, then the turning point for my anger. I developed empathy for human beings whose work is so demanding and demeaning that they must be turned into automatons with numbers instead of names. I learned that bumping into situations and people who cause anger is unavoidable. It's just a part of life. Even though it seems much more horrible when you are tired and full of frustration and sorrow yourself.

"One of the ways we can deal with it is to take control of ourselves and our thinking and our emotions The other is to play the cowboy bit and just punch them in the nose, which is a quick way to reach forgiveness because then the situation is quickly ended. My advice is to get the issue resolved as quickly as possible. Then move on.

"Finally I learned that I can only forgive myself for harboring any type of animosity against anyone, including the system. Remember when I threw the rocks in the ravine in order to release my resentments, and you wrote about it in "Throwing Stones" in your book *Soulwork*? Well I know this process helped you and a lot of other people. It helped me too. When I threw the rocks, it was more of a release from my own shortcomings at not understanding where the other person was coming from. That's what I thought about for a long time before releasing the rocks. In effect, I forgave myself.

"We all know that harboring anger is detrimental to one's physical, emotional, and mental health. So get the anger issue resolved as quickly as possible, That's my advice. And don't forget to throw the stones. Hope this will help someone else who is going through what I went through.

"Forgiveness works!"

PREVENTIVE FORGIVENESS

Another friend, who, like so many of my contemporaries, had been involved for years with family needs and family caregiving, when asked for her comments on forgiveness, gave me an intriguing answer.

"I think that one of the things that's most important to do, when faced with caregiving, especially long-term, especially with someone you love so much and who depends on you, is to practice what I call preventive forgiveness. That's when you have a good talk with yourself, or sometimes several solitary conversations along the way, in which you remind yourself that no matter how much you love the person you are caring for, and no matter how much that person loves you, that there is no way that you can meet all their needs. You cannot heal them, you cannot save them, you cannot make them happy, you cannot carry the pain and the fear for them. You are not responsible for THEIR final journey and how they take it. Oh that's a hard lesson to learn!

"What I suggest is that for your own health and sanity (we all know the stories of the caregivers who keel over and die BEFORE the ones they are caring for), for your own peace of mind, that you practice preventive forgiveness. That's when you forgive yourself now, today, every day for a while if needs be, for NOT being able to meet all the needs of the person you love. There's a lot of talk these days about setting boundaries. Well good luck to you if you can do that in a long-term caregiving situation. I have very, very seldom found that the caregivers don't give enough. They give and give and give. But you know what? It's never enough. It can't be. The needs are too great. So you have to forgive yourself ahead of time, seventy times seven, if necessary, so that you CAN go on, so that you CAN help. Get over your guilt fast. It's false guilt.

"The truth is, no matter what you do, there's still going to be grief. There's still going to be remorse. There's still going to be the memories. The fatigue fades. The 'if-onlys' will tear you apart if you let them.

"Preventive forgiveness. Living and loving with an open, compassionate heart. And knowing you did the best you could. And it was enough."

"Implicit in forgiving God is an acceptance of forces in the universe that are part of the great mystery of life, which we cannot ultimately understand, control or predict."

ROBIN CASARJIAN

CHAPTER ELEVEN

• • • •

Forgiving God

Some stories defy categorization. Some stories are so unusual, so bizarre, so mystifying, that the person who tells the story is changed at depth, and the person who hears the story is changed as well. This happened to me a few years ago when I lived in L.A. and had the opportunity to meet many people from many walks of life, especially in the grief support groups I facilitated and participated in.

A woman about my own age, who had also come from the South originally, became a dear friend. We spent many hours reminiscing about the differences in the culture and times we were brought up in, as contrasted to the freer, more emotionally accessible atmosphere we now shared.

One day after a particularly grueling grief support group, we went out to dinner and talked for hours. She then told me of the most extraordinary event that had ever happened to her. "Don't tell my name," she said, "But someday, tell my story." Here it is, in her own words.

"You know, sometimes something so incredible happens in your life that you can remember it as if watching it unfold, in perfect clarity and intense recollection, before your very eyes. Well I'll never forget what happened to me when I went for a week-long seminar to Acapulco, Mexico, to take part in a dream workshop that I felt sure would help me not only in my own counseling work with others, but in my own growth and development. At the time, I felt over-burdened and overworked, with some minor health problems and a continuing weight problem that I put down to stress and my own grief, which I was still struggling with as the years passed. In fact, I was in therapy myself at the time. I mention all this to kind of set the scene for what happened next.

"At the workshop, I met the fourteen strangers in the group, which was led by a male psychotherapist who was also an ex-priest, as well as by a warm and wonderful woman about my own age who was a Jungian analyst. So the stage was set for a deep and fruitful week of great inner exploration through our dreams and our images. We all stayed in a beautiful villa overlooking the Bay, run by an expatriate New York woman who had settled in Acapulco for reasons of her own, and who was now involved with one of the two bartenders who worked for her at the resort, either Luis or Jorge, I was not sure which. It was a beautiful and relaxed setting, with all of us meeting twice a day for sessions, three times a day for shared meals around a huge outdoor table on the patio, and individual times for reflection and journal writing.

"I shared a room on an outdoor screened-in porch with a woman of Greek descent. There were people there from all walks of life, an angry black, female college administra-tor, two artists, a young gay man, a husband and wife, very mild-mannered and extremely depressed, a smattering of health professionals, a writer, a librarian, a theologian. Their ages ranged from late twenties to late sixties. I don't know what I expected. What I found was a melting pot of other people's emotions, other people's insights and issues, other people opening to their own unresolved pain and grief. Everyone but me.

"I had always been an active dreamer, and kept a pad at my bedside to record my dreams each night. We were instructed to do so again. But for some reason I couldn't remember any of my dreams. Anything I did write down in the middle of the night read like scrawled gibberish the next morning.

"Let me explain the layout of the place a bit further. It's important. The room I shared with my Greek roommate was on the third floor of the three-story villa, which was built on terraces that sloped down to a pool and the sea. On the other side there was cleared land and then the encroaching tropical jungle. We were some way out of town, although little villages existed nearby. My room could only be reached by a winding stair that led to two sets of rooms, one shared by three other women at the conference, and the one that I shared with my new acquaintance. There were no real doors, only swinging wooden panels. My roommate took the bed nearest the swinging doors, the bed in between us was vacant, and my own bed was in a corner near the attached bathroom. Everything was very open, unlocked, and designed so that the breezes would blow through the sultry and oppressive heat-laden air.

"As the days passed, I found myself more and more distressed, seemingly unable to connect to the other participants and their intimate revelations. I became a quiet observer, which is not my style at all. I decided to treat the workshop as a much-needed vacation, and trust that any insights would come to me later.

"But then one night at supper, the owner of the villa announced that a medicine man, an Indian shaman, was coming to meet the group. She had heard this via the grapevine in the kitchen, and like a proud hostess presenting show and tell to amuse her guests, she offered us the medicine man as our evening entertainment.

"'Everyone calls him Don Chuy,' she told us, 'And we should be respectful of him, as he has lived and practiced his medicine ways around here for many years.'

"As she spoke, a small, wiry, wizened figure appeared out of the shadows of the trees and onto the lighted veranda. Don Chuy was less than five feet tall, dressed in a pair of shorts and a man's white shirt, with sandals on his gnarled bony feet. He was the color of pecan wood, with a head of magnificent white hair, a mouth full of gold teeth, an infectious chuckle, a merry grin, and large black sparkling eyes. He spoke only Spanish, so the owner of the villa translated as best she could. He carried a long walking stick in one hand, taller than he was. It seemed to be made of some indigenous hardwood, and was as gnarled and polished and brown as he was. It was adorned with feathers and shells that blew and clanked in the evening breeze. He also carried a woven bag full, I surmised, of the tools of his trade. I could not take my eyes off of him. I was mesmerized by this small strange wise man.

"We all stood and bowed to the medicine man. But since I was the only one in the group, besides the owner of the villa, who spoke any Spanish, I engaged him in conversation in my halting and rusty schoolroom Spanish. He came straight to me and beamed at me. I remember in the back of my mind thinking, 'This is why I came here, to meet the shaman.' After a few pleasantries, the others in the group drifted over to the outdoor bar, and Don Chuy and I were left alone. We sat on the terraced steps and talked for a little while. I don't remember what we said. But there was an extraordinary connection between us. Like electricity. I felt that this aged peasant knew secrets about me that I did not even know. I felt that I could learn from this man. I asked what I could do to continue our association. With a twinkle in his eyes, he invited me to participate in a cleansing healing ritual. I assented.

"The next afternoon, he came to my room and performed a private and strange ritual that involved smudge sticks and sweet-smelling oils, and chanting. He asked me some personal questions and I answered them in my halting Spanish. I could understand everything that he said, but I was not sure if he understood me. One question I remembered him asking me was. 'And who takes care of you?' I answered with a burst of tears and a shake of my head. In any other context, all this would have seemed extremely bizarre. But in this place and with this tiny, elfin wise man, it seemed as though all he did and all he said was absolutely clear and true, and that the rest of my life, my outer life elsewhere, was the dream.

"After the cleansing healing ritual was completed, he told me to rest. He also told me that whatever happened within the next three days, was for my healing and for my clearing. He said that he would watch over me, and not to worry about the dark dreams and shapes that might come to me in the night, that he would be there. I then asked him what I owed him. He told me nothing, that it was his pleasure to serve. I offered then to assist him as a translator in other healing sessions with other members of the group. He told me that it was not necessary. That I was the one he had come to see. I presented him with a gift, since he would take no money. It was an elaborate woven bag I had brought with me from an earlier trip I had taken to another part of the world. He was delighted with this gift. His smile lit up his face and the whole room. He literally danced with joy. He then began to transfer all his possessions into this new bag I had given him. Then he bowed and left the room.

"After I had rested for a while, I began to write down all my impressions of the shaman and the strange and comforting session I had participated in. I felt a sense of anticipation, of waiting, of being suspended in time. I vowed that whatever happened, I would never forget the sense of energy that this man had brought into my life.

"It was now only three days before we were to return to the United States. I spent those days in a peaceful, waiting reverie, and although my nights were troubled by dark and swirling dreams, I remembered what Don Chuy had said, and did not let them frighten me. Sometimes when I opened my eyes in the middle of the night, I thought I could see his bent figure sleeping in a corner of the room. But it must have been my imagination. Once another of the workshop participants remarked that she kept tripping on the figure of the old man outside the swinging doors of my bedroom, and wondered if he followed me everywhere or just didn't have a place to sleep. Sometimes I did see him, either eating in the kitchen and joking with the staff, or standing on the edge of the jungle, there where the cleared spaces ended and the primitive growth began, there with his staff in his hand.

"Meanwhile, the other participants went on analyzing their dreams and meeting in spontaneous groups without benefit of Don Chuy's special skills. The night before we were to leave for the United States, we had a special party to celebrate the week of the workshop. There was lots of dancing and laughter and some participants drank more than usual. Soon everyone in the party decided to go to town and dance at a nightclub. Since I did not drink, and was rather weary, I decided to stay at the villa. My roommate decided to stay too, and we both turned in early. The next day would be full, with one more group session and an afternoon flight out of Acapulco. I was already packed, as was she.

"The night was quiet and still. I could hear my roommate snoring softly in her bed near the door. I lay in the darkness, drowsy, at peace or so I thought, with the entire trip, no matter that no earth-shattering results had appeared for me. Meeting with the shaman had been the high point of the trip. I must have drifted off to sleep.

"Sometime around midnight, I was aware of a dark shape in the room. Something had awakened me. The hairs on my neck lifted. I could not breathe. I felt a hand on my leg, traveling upwards. Then a drunken male figure swayed over me. His other hand held something cold and dark against my neck. I could not breathe. I could not scream. He asked me in slurred Spanish if I wanted to have a party with him. At first I could not see who it was. An atavistic fear stirred deep inside me. I had been here before! Never again!

"The light from the moon poured in through the enclosed porch slanting windows. I could now see that the figure by my bed was one of the two bartenders at the resort, the one who was, or so I thought, romantically

128

involved with the owner. I couldn't remember his name. Luis? Jorge? With a muffled cry I kicked at him with all my might, rolled out of bed onto the floor, dislodging his hands. Then I began screaming for help. My roommate, who had been asleep, sat up in bed and turned on the lamp. The intruder stood swaying and surly next to my bed. He kept on whining in Spanish that he just wanted to have a party with me.

"My roommate and I realized that for the first time since we had arrived at the villa, we were alone except for this large, drunken lumbering man. The staff had gone back to their homes for their Saturday night off. The owner and all the guests were in town dancing. Only she and I remained, in an unlocked room at the top of the villa. We began to call for help.

"Suddenly I saw a light outside of our windows. It was a swinging kerosene lantern. It was Don Chuy! He beamed and waved at us and began to climb the stairs. I noticed then that the drunken bartender had a large dark bottle in one hand. It was this that I had felt pressed against my neck and throat, while his other hand had traveled up my leg. Then Don Chuy appeared through the swinging doors. He must have weighed less then one hundred pounds, while the bartender was well over six feet tall and at least two hundred pounds. The two men stared at one another.

"'Party,' muttered the bartender. 'I just want to have a party.'

"'Go down to the kitchen now, Luis,' said Don Chuy firmly. 'You are frightening these ladies.'

"The large man nodded. Incredibly, he obeyed. He lurched toward the door and stumbled down the stairs. We stared after his retreating figure.

"'I am sorry that I was not here to sleep by your door,' said Don Chuy serenely. 'I had gone to see my cousin, who is ill. But I am back now, and all is well. There will be no more trouble tonight.'

"My roommate and I were still frightened and wide awake. We discussed the incident in hushed tones. 'Why didn't he come to my bed instead of yours?' she wondered. 'He had to go past me and the empty bed to get to yours.' We were both middle-aged and definitely non-seductive. Neither of us had encouraged the bartender. We had no intimation of any trouble. We had gone to bed unafraid, even though there were no locks on the door, no way to keep anyone out. We each grabbed up the water bottles by our beds, as if to use them as weapons should the intruder return. I can still see us there, with all the lights on, with our water bottles at the ready, talking in hushed tones about the incident.

"Don Chuy meanwhile, settled himself outside our door and put his head on his woven bag, as if to go to sleep. Just then we heard noise and laughter and the slam of car doors and realized that the workshop participants and the owner of the villa were returning from the town. Don Chuy went down to explain what had happened. Someone led Luis off to his own quarters, after a heated exchange.

"And then, incredibly, it was all over. The night closed in again. Everyone went back to sleep. Except me. My heart raced in the darkness. I, who had never been afraid to be alone at night, I who had raised my children alone as a single parent and kept the bogeyman from THEIR beds, I who.... Suddenly a wave of memories swept over me. Memories I had blocked from consciousness for thirty years. Things I had never told anyone, not my friends, not fellow counselors, not my therapist, not anyone. Not even Don Chuy. Shaking and trembling in my bed, I relived, moment by moment, a time thirty years before. I was a single parent raising small children alone in a traditional southern town in the mid-sixties.

"One summer night, a man I knew, a man I had even dated briefly, before deciding he was not the man I wanted in my life, had come to my door right after I had tucked my children into their beds. I had answered the door, still dressed in my work clothes, but tired and grimy and ready for bed. My acquaintance then explained that his truck had broken down a block away, and that he needed to call for a tow. Remembering that I lived in the neighborhood, he took a chance that I was up and asked politely if he could use the phone. No one ever locked their doors back then, but I had latched my screen door. I will never forget unlatching that screen door and letting him in. I remember that it was a beautiful summer evening, very like the one I was experiencing now, as I lay in my bed at the villa. The screened in porch had the same kind of wood that was on the screen doors, both back and front, at my house so many years ago, in a time and place I wanted only to forget. And had succeeded in forgetting. Until now.

"The man I knew briefly then came into the house. He was smiling. I pointed to the phone and turned to go back into another room. He grabbed my leg. I remembered so well that he grabbed my leg as I turned to leave. It knocked me off balance. I went down onto the wooden hall floor. The man I knew, the man I once had dated, the man I thought was a friend, shoved a gun at my head. I couldn't see the gun. I could only feel it. It was cold and hard. It pressed into my neck and the side of my head.

"'If you say a word I'll blow your head off,' he said. I remember thinking, just don't let him near the children. But I had to get away. I kicked at him with my other foot. I knocked him off balance. He had been crouching over me. I crawled on my hands and knees through the dark. I wanted to close and lock the door to the children's room. I wanted to escape. I wanted God to help me. I wanted this nightmare to be over. I wanted,—oh I wanted everything but this fear.

"I guess he knew what I was doing. I guess he too didn't want to wake the children. I remember thinking, If I can get to the side door, I can escape. But then he would be in the house alone with my children. And he would hurt them.

I knew he would hurt them. I saw the side door. I could be free. Then I heard another door opening. It was the door to my children's room. The man slipped through the door into their bedroom. He whispered to me, 'Come here.' It was like a game. I remembered thinking that it was like a terrible game that he had set up and that he knew how the game would come out because he was the hunter. I was his prey. If I went out the door, I would be safe and could call for help. If I ran away, my children would die.

"The man laughed. He was drunk or on pills of some kind, or both. He was crazy. I got to my feet. I could still make a run for it. The door to the bedroom opened wider. I looked in. The man pointed his gun at the head of my sleeping son, who was only about six years old.

"'You can go or you can stay,' he whispered. 'Doesn't matter any way.'

"I was afraid to take a step. I was afraid the children would wake up. I was unbearably, utterly filled with fear.

"The man laughed. He knew me. He knew my children.

"'What do you want?' I asked him. 'I'll do whatever you want.'

"He crossed to the door, stepped out into the hall, closed the door behind him. He put his arms around me. 'I want to have a party,' he said. 'That's all. I just want to have a party.'

"I remember that he led me back to my bedroom. I

remember that he never let go of the gun. I remember the feel of the gun against the side of my head and neck there beside me on the pillow. I remember, now I remembered— the brutal rape.

"Finally it was over. 'If you ever say a word to anyone,' he whispered in the dark, 'I'll come back and blow your children's heads off.' I knew he meant what he said. I had forgotten. I had forgotten that this brutal event had ever happened. I remembered now. I remembered lying there and thinking so many thoughts, thoughts like 'Where are you, God?' And 'At least my children are safe.' And 'I will never trust anyone again.' And then the litany would start all over again and again and again. 'Where are you, God? You are not in this room. You did not save me. You did not take care of me, God. There is no one to take care of me.'

"I never again saw the man who had raped me. Why didn't I go to the police? It was different back then, where I lived. There were no rape crisis centers, there were no counselors for battered women, there was no understand- ing. I knew the man. I had let him into my house at night. There were no witnesses. And I couldn't take the chance that he would come back and hurt my children. I could NOT take the chance. I did nothing. I buried the assault deep within me. I told no one.

"Now, thirty years later, I knew what I had come to Mexico for. I had come to be healed of my nightmare. I had come to be healed of my past. Luis was the trigger that

134

brought it all flooding back.

"The next day I tried to tell my story in the last group session before we left the villa. It was important to me to have someone hear me, to recognize just what I had gone through, to understand that the choices I had made so many years ago were choices that led to other choices, that led to stoicism, to mistrust, to fear, to buried, horrifying pain. I don't know to this day if the other workshop participants comprehended what I had gone through. My roommate and two other women were sympathetic. I remember throwing up all the next day, while they held me, throwing up the pain of that long-ago time.

"'But I had to save my children,' I kept saying. 'I did the only thing I could.' It was important to me that they understand and agree with me. 'But where was God when I needed him?' I kept saying. 'God abandoned me. I will never trust God again.'

"There were really too many memories for me to handle at one time. A deep and fearful wound had been opened within me. For some reason, the men in the workshop, including and especially the group leader, seemed opaque to me. Closed off, as if they not only didn't understand, but didn't want to understand. 'The only one who would understand,' I thought to myself, 'is Don Chuy. He had a hand in this. In some way, he knew this was going to happen. He knew and was the catalyst for my healing.'

"I went to the kitchen to thank him for his help and to

say good-bye. My heart welled with gratitude for this gift he had given me. The gift of healing the wound of the past, the gift of coming back to myself. I could not find him. I asked for him in my halting Spanish. The cook shook her head. 'He has gone back to his village,' she said.

"'No,' I insisted, tears in my eyes. 'He was right here, you know, the small man, the old man, the medicine man, Don Chuy.'

"'Ah Señora,' she said, shaking her head. 'You should not call him so by that name. It is not respectful. He is a holy man. You do not call him so.'

"'Just give me his full name and address so that I may write to him and send him something, ' I asked her. 'I am leaving on the plane in fifteen minutes. It is urgent that I contact him.'

"'His name, Señora, he is called Don Jesús de la Paz. He has no address. Everyone knows him around here. He goes back to his village and comes and goes again, when he is needed. I do not know when he will appear again.'

"But I did not hear the rest of what she was saying. 'His name is Don Jesus de la Paz. His name is Jesus of Peace,' I translated. Where was God when I needed him? He was in this place and I did not know him.

"A mystical medicine man named Jesus of Peace had come to me in this foreign land, opened up the caverns of past pain within me, and rescued me. I could no longer doubt that God works in mysterious ways.

"So I came back to L.A., and told my therapist the story and with his help, worked through the rest of the pain and mistrust. But I have never forgotten Don Chuy, Don Jesús de la Paz, and the part he played in healing a thirty-year old trauma.

"My whole life changed after that. In ways profound and mysterious and lasting. In ways that seem as mysterious as that time in Acapulco, when a buried nightmare became reality, triggered me into remembering and releasing, and led me into forgiveness and peace. The reverberations of that encounter with Don Chuy and the resolution of my bitter distrust of God are still with me. I had blamed myself for letting the man I knew as a friend into my house. I had blamed the man and in a sense all men for the brutal rape, I had blamed the times and the circumstances in which I lived that I had needed to keep silent and live in fear. There was even a part of me that had blamed my innocent children for forcing me to choose between their safety and mine. Most of all, I had blamed God.

"So my forgiveness started with myself and radiated outward. Until it changed my life. When you are holding secrets of such magnitude inside, how can you find peace? I couldn't. I didn't know what peace and safety were. But now I do.

"I never went back to Acapulco. I never contacted Don Chuy again. But even as I tell you this story, I can see his slight, wiry figure before me, the white head gleaming, the black eyes dancing, the staff quivering in his hand. And I know that I was given a gift of great power. I was given the gift of myself. I was given the gift of my own life back. I was given the chance to reenact and remember, in a small way, the nightmare I had been through. A chance to resolve and release it. And all because of an old mysterious magical man named Don Jesús de la Paz.

"One way in which that encounter changed my life is how I am able to help the people who come to me. Somehow I can be the catalyst for their healing, just as Don Chuy was the catalyst for mine. I can be in the space of their unremembered pain. I can hold the space for resolution. I can show them that I care for them, will take care of them for that moment as they remember and relive their pain.

"I remember that a woman came to me whose mother had been murdered by a young man in her neighborhood, the paper boy or a delivery boy, some young kid on drugs. She could not comprehend why or how such a horrible thing could have happened. She was a mother herself, and a doctor as well. She had always been in charge of her life. The horror of the experience was beyond her comprehension.

"All the wise men and sages of all the ages have asked the same question she asked, 'How could such a terrible thing happen?'

"Sometimes there are no answers. Sometimes the only answer is that we do not know. But that as we learn to forgive the unforgivable, in others, in the world, the unforgivable becomes forgivable. Sometimes it takes thirty years. Sometimes it takes far less. But out of that compassion and empathy that the daughter of the murdered woman felt, she was able to be more open, more real, more compassionate to the hurting people in her care.

"Sometimes we are broken open and in the breaking open, even if we do not understand it at the time, a healing comes that brings us closer to resolution, to peace, to God. It is a mysterious process, one that I am only beginning to understand. But when I deal with people who are in great grief and suffering, I am there for them. I know. I hear. I recognize. I acknowledge. I understand. And no one has to keep the unforgivable inside them for thirty years.

"It's really amazing, when you think about it, that so many of us do hold great anger and resentment against God. Or whatever we perceive God to be within the context of our belief system and our faith. I am convinced, however, that a part of finding our way home, to wholeness and peace and trust, is in forgiving God."

"We are not really angry at God. We are angry at ourselves because we have not mastered our divinity yet. Our divinity is realized through forgiveness. It is the unconditional love for ourselves that we are seeking. Forgive Self=Forgive God. They are the same."

ROBIN CASARJIAN

CHAPTER TWELVE

••••

Hating God And Loving God

There are times when I wish that I knew all the secrets of the ages, that I was a wise theologian, that I was privy to the mysterious workings of the human heart and the full truth of the spiritual lessons that all of us are faced with as we continue our journeys toward forgiveness, toward enlightenment, toward home.

Recently I interviewed a woman who wanted to share her journey from hating God to loving God. Yet when I mentioned the text of the interview to another friend of mine, she was aghast.

"You can't write about people hating God," she said. "That's wicked."

No. That's human.

Sometimes those of us who feel most deeply the pain of the world and the pain of our own place within the world, sometimes those of us who want so desperately to heal ourselves and help others, first have to come face to face with our own deep feelings. And when we talk about how we have been abandoned, or wounded, or abused, or denigrated, or forced to endure great losses in our lives, sometimes we say, not aloud, but to ourselves. "How could God have

141

done this to me?" And then the corollary, "God does not love me, so how can I love Him?" And then the next sentence comes tumbling out, "I hate you, God!" Yes.

The woman I interviewed who had the love-hate relationship with God wanted to share her story. She wanted to tell her truth. It took courage and wisdom to do so. Here is her story:

"I never knew my birth mother. I never even heard my birth father mentioned. I was told at an early age that my mother, who was sixteen, pregnant, and unmarried, had abandoned me. I was raised in a strict, cold, unfeeling household by conscientious, rigid, adoptive parents. I was made to feel again and again, that I should be grateful to them for raising me. My brother, also adopted, felt the same way I did. No matter the food on the table or the clothes on our back, there was such an air of criticism and coldness, that we both went within ourselves in order to survive.

"Now that I am an adult, I can see my adoptive parents with more compassion. But at the time, I felt that I had no identity. I felt that I did not exist. I felt that I did not deserve to exist. I felt deep shame at being born and being unwanted. My way of handling this as a child was to go within and withdraw my feelings from the world. I found a diary recently when I was going through some old things of mine. I had written again and again in it, 'Why doesn't God love me? Why doesn't anyone love me? If you don't love me, I won't love you! I hate you, God.' All this in an eight-year-old scrawl. I burst into tears when I saw the words I had written as a child.

"As a teenager, I became very rebellious. It was my way of getting someone, anyone to notice me. Oh I went through such agonies as a child and young adult. But even in my rebellion, I ended up following the path my adoptive parents had prescribed. I made good grades, I went to college, I became an accountant. I held everything within me. I didn't let anyone get close to me. I decided not to have children. How could I love a tiny human being when I couldn't love myself? When I didn't know how to love? When I couldn't trust God? I went through a number of surgeries as well, always, always trying to find some way to heal the pain within my body, my emotions and my soul.

"Finally, as I approached thirty, I began to search, not for my lost birth mother or father, not for my roots. I began to search for myself. I was, fortunately, married to a man who is my best friend. And when I began to explore music, (which I had abandoned as a career choice in order to be an accountant), I found a profound connection. It was as if the music I studied, played, or heard, brought me to the core of myself. I began to explore everything from art to gardening to Yoga to meditation. I studied anthropology. I studied various alternative healing paths. I even became an assistant midwife in order to connect with the deep rhythms of giving birth and the bonding, mothering connection. Each path I studied led me deeper into the core of my self.

"Yet I still felt like I had no identity. That underneath all the old rage and shame and pain and grief, there was only more rage and pain and shame and grief. I realized that I had never learned to pray. I had only learned to hate. In my meditations and in my therapeutic work, I began to soften, to gradually and safely let the rage and pain and shame and guilt (guilt even for being born, I now realize!) up and out into the light. I began to feel the patterns of my being, not to just see them intellectually. I realized that I had a lot of forgiving to do. But how? And where to start? I could now be compassionate with the birthing mothers I was encountering. But could I be compassionate toward my own birth mother? Could I be trust that my own birth had meaning? Could I trust that my life now had meaning? I pondered all these questions.

"Yet I still could not feel safe enough to begin to feel. I committed myself to a year of intense therapeutic healing. And what happened within the safety and compassion of therapy was that I could finally say, 'I hate you, God.' Like the little girl who wrote in her diary the same words so many years ago, I came face to face with my own hatred. And then I realized that since I am created by God, and have a spark of God within me, that if I hated God, for any reason at all, justified or unjustified, then I was hating myself. And that the core of my deep problems of shame and alienation was my hatred and non-forgiveness of myself. Of course there were many people I needed to forgive, from that sixteen-year-old birth mother, the unknown and uncaring birth father, the adoptive parents who had done the best they knew how with their own stunted sense of caring.

"But first I had to come face to face with my emotions toward God. It is so painful and yet so freeing for me to admit that I hated God. Because it was a giant step in realizing that I also LOVED God as well. That in back of the presumed hatred was the yearning to be at peace and to be loved. Beyond the pain was the yearning to be loved and accepted and cared for by God. And for that to happen, for me to know it as a possibility, I had to learn, like a child learns, how to love and accept myself. I'm still learning that.

"But I wanted to share my story, because I think that it is so important for people to know that on the other side of 'I hate you, God' is 'I forgive you, God,' and then 'I love you, God.' And then 'I know you love me, God.' And then 'I am one with your love and caring and safety and peace, God.' So now I feel like a wondrous child who has discovered a new best friend. Who has discovered that the face of love is no longer turned away from her. I'm still learning to forgive. It starts with me, and radiates outward."

My friend was convinced that her case was not unusual. That if people are honest with themselves, there is often doubt and mistrust and a feeling of abandonment by God. There is often a sense of "My God, my God, why has Thou forsaken me?"

It is what we DO when we stumble upon this hatred held deep within our hearts that matters. Do we deny that we are anything but sweetness and light? Or can we be courageous enough to own our deepest and most private and most unacceptable feelings and THEN by recognizing, acknowledging, meditation and prayer, action, understanding and awareness, come finally and trustfully to healing and change? I think we can. Some would protest that of course we are loved by God, and of course God does not kill our loved ones, allow rape and abuse, reject us or abandon us to a cold and unloving life when we are too helpless to fend for ourselves.

And yet. And yet. To those of us going through the losses of life, whether as child or adult, arguing God's providence and beneficence is a futile exercise. We must come through the dark in order to recognize and feel and accept the light.

My friend feels, as does the woman who was raped, and the woman whose mother was murdered, that she can no longer blame God for human horror. She can no longer blame God for loss or despair. But first she had to own the reality of her own deep feelings of abandonment.

Sometimes the horror seems incomprehensible to human hearts. When the tragic Oklahoma City bombing of the federal building happened on April 19, 1995, in which over 170 people, including many children, were killed randomly and senselessly as a "protest" by American terrorists, the world was stunned. Again and again people asked the same questions. "How could this happen? How could God allow such a thing to happen?" The world also watched as extraordinary images of human valor and human kindness swept the country. Along with the TV images of death and random destruction, were pictures of courage, caring, and unshakable faith. The nation grieved together with the families. The nation prayed together with the families.

A wise and devout friend of mine, who watched the families of the murdered victims as they coped with their tragedy, had this to say. "This is an event in time that will tell the world what real spiritual strength is. This is what faith is. This is what courage is. This is what dignity and nobility in the face of human loss is." She went on to remind me of the man who said, when interviewed at the site where his loved ones died, that he couldn't blame God for this tragedy, because he needed God so much to get THROUGH this tragedy. And there was the woman who said that God had his arms around her to get her through, and that God, in his mercy and love, also had his arms around her grandchildren who had died.

We may never know why something this tragic happens. But out of even senseless horror comes the deepest heroism of the human heart.

Perhaps it is only when we have gone through the dark night of the soul that we can consciously and prayerfully

147

rebuild our relationship to God. No matter how difficult or impossible it seems at the time, we CAN learn to trust again. And from that deepened trust, reach out to others with increased compassion and strength.

"I had to forgive myself, before I could forgive God," says my friend.

"I had to forgive my rapist before I could forgive God," says another.

"I had to forgive my mother's murderer before I could forgive God," says another.

And there are other tales as well. "I had to forgive the plane crash that killed my brother."

"I had to forgive the disease that killed my son."

"I had to forgive the earthquake, the flood, the tornado, the hurricane, the fire that took my loved ones from me."

And how DO we forgive the incomprehensible? The act of nature, the act of fate, the act of madmen, the act that seems, in our limited human understanding, to be an act of God? Step by step. We continue to forgive what we can and however we can, even in the face of the unknown, even in the face of helplessness, even in the face of horror. We continue to forgive.

The seven steps of forgiveness have a cumulative effect. Like rushing water that cannot be contained and outruns its banks in order to spill over into the surrounding countryside, like clear water that starts as a trickle and becomes a roaring stream, a waterfall, a cleansing path opens up before us when we forgive God. Then we become a part of the cleansing healing stream. And we overflow our lives in joy and forgiveness.

"Spiritual partners commit to a growing dynamic. Their commitment is truly a promise toward their own growth, to their own spiritual survival and not to their physical."

GARY ZUKAV

CHAPTER THIRTEEN

....

Finding True Love
After Forgiveness

Along with the stories of sorrow and the stories of horror, along with the stories of triumph over tragedy and lessons hard-won, of dark nights of the soul and the morning after, no story has touched my heart more deeply than a dual interview I conducted with an old friend of mine, a man who has gone through years of forgiveness and soul-searching, and a beautiful woman named Judy, who, as she told me her incredible story, shed light on the steps that she took from incomprehensible tragedy to a new life with an old friend, the man she now loves.

When I first spoke to Judy, I was struck by her beauty, her calmness, and her sense of self. Sometimes tears would well up from the depths of her eyes, but she was clear, poised, and reflective as she slowly filled in her story:

"The hardest thing for me to forgive is my husband's suicide after our marriage of eleven years. My children and I still don't understand why. There were no signs. We saw nothing. Others in my support group say that they can pinpoint signs, but here there was no warning. My daughter came home from Colorado for three weeks to visit, and even she didn't notice anything unusual. My husband had just started a new business. Things were finally going well for us after many years of ups and downs. Things were on the upswing. In the past, he would get very depressed, and often went for counseling to alleviate the terror he felt from things that had happened to him in his past, mostly from the time when he was in Vietnam. He couldn't talk about it. Not to me. Just in counseling.

"One day he went and borrowed a gun from his brother-in-law. His brother-in-law didn't think anything of this, because Mike told him he was going into a bad part of town. He was a used-car wholesaler and often had to visit areas of the city that were not safe. In this part of the country, you'd be amazed how many people carry guns.

"Mike drove to the lake outside of town, and approximately at sunset, shot himself in the head. He left a letter for me and for his two girls. He told us that he loved us and that none of this was anyone's fault, that no one had caused his pain, that no one was to blame, but that he couldn't be the person he wanted to be, and that he couldn't go on any longer. Much earlier in the marriage there had been some martial problems. We sought help for those. But now we were doing all right. We were doing all right!" She shook her head in disbelief.

"I just can't understand it. His kids from his previous marriage had just graduated from college, he was reunited with his daughters, one even came to live with us. No one suspected anything was wrong. He was a successful sales manager and car wholesaler at a car dealership. I worked in marketing as well. We had a shared history and mutual friends and good grown children. So you would think that we were doing all the right things. Yet my husband's father died the day after Mike and I got married. I don't know if he ever got over that. It cast a pall over our marriage for a while. There may still have been unresolved problems from that time."

"Who did you have to forgive?"

"Everyone and everything, especially God. Oh how I hated God for this huge, additional challenge in my life! I didn't know which was worse. Mike's death or the death of my previous husband from lung cancer. I have had so many losses in a row. I am still reeling from this latest loss."

"Are you still working through forgiveness?"

"Yes. There are stages of grief. It's a roller coaster. You think you're almost healed, then your emotions trigger back to earlier stages. I often go to the door or answer the phone or go to the mailbox to see if there is a message from Mike. Something to help me understand why he took his own life. Grief and shock take so many forms. And it takes so long to heal. I'm still learning that. Just as I am still learning for-giveness of these tragedies that I have been witness to, that I have been involved in, that I have been a part of."

"Once I read something so absurd," I told her. "It was

a book by a minister in which he stated that it takes a minimum of forty-eight hours to get over grief. Just forty-eight hours! When I read that, I laughed until I cried. Try forty-eight weeks, forty-eight months. Try years. Until you have been through deep loss and tragedy, you will never know what it feels like. You can't measure grief. You can't hurry grief. It takes its own sweet time. It can't be forced or denied. You just go on one day at a time."

"I agree" said Judy. "My tendency is to put too much pressure on myself. I want to be finished with grief. I must give my self time. I must forgive the self. I think I SHOULD be through this. Reading consoling books helps, also being with caring friends and family, also my support group and my counseling with another therapist. Everything helps. But it's so hard."

"How do you find the courage to go on?"

"Someone helps you through ... God gets you through. You can't do it on your own. There's too much to do. There's daily living and the people in your life as well. I also had to deal with my husband's business and my career. When something like this happens, you find out who are your close friends. I have found that many people are afraid of death, afraid to be around in case they catch it—death. So they avoid you.

"That's what happened in my previous marriage.

"I took care of my previous husband, Claude, a police officer, for one-and-a-half years when he had cancer. He for six months. He went to California. He told me he wanted to find himself before he died. Those six months, I didn't know if he was alive or dead. He came back when he was ready to die. He was on his deathbed. I was his primary caregiver. His strength. I missed that important time with him, that last six months we could have had together. He came back a month before he died. He died on Thanksgiving Day. He died at home. There was a lot of blood. It was from a hemorrhage. It was a violent end (his lung cancer).

"When the police walked in, they thought he had been murdered—there was so much so much blood. But the police chief's wife lived only four doors down from me. She was on the dispatcher radio and heard the call. She came over immediately to vouch for the truth of what had happened. She told the police Claude wasn't murdered—he had cancer.

"I though I'd never get over that death. When I close my eyes, I can still see the scene."

"How have you managed to trust again?"

"I am a caring person. I am willing to risk loving again. I have come to new levels of trust through each stage in my life.

"Yet I am still healing from the first death. I had to forgive Claude for being ill and dying and leaving me. Just as I have to forgive Mike for killing himself and leaving me. It takes a lot of soul-searching through the pain to recover my own sense of self."

"What do your children think about all that has happened?"

"My children tell me that they have learned from my courage. All that we've been through together unites us as a family. My son Michael says that everything that we have gone through has made us not harder but tougher and stronger. You grow another layer, another skin. But sometimes I wonder what is waiting around the corner. Yet I just have to trust."

"How do you keep yourself well?"

"Sometimes I can't. Sometimes it just gets to be too much. I became very ill after Mike died. I took a long look at death myself. I kept on losing weight. I finally came out of it. There's something in life I haven't accomplished yet. Something yet to do. This keeps me going. Maybe my new relationship. This friend of so many years who has come back into my life ... I think I'll keep him." We laughed together and the tears fled from her eyes.

"This new relationship is a big surprise to me. It came out of the clear blue sky. He is an old friend, a counselor to our family in various capacities for many years. He knows our family history. I believe in angels. So does he. They are looking after us. I have a stronger relationship with God since Richard and I met again. Richard is a big part of that, because of his strong faith in God. I used to ask 'Where were you, God, when I needed you?' Now I see that He was there all the time. Through the worst times and now through the best times.

"I am a sales and marketing manager for a large national company. I'm doing well professionally. But now I am changing my life in an astounding way. I have quit my job. I am selling my home, the home where I experienced the grief and loss of my two husbands, and Richard and I are moving to Colorado to start over again in the small town where my daughter and her husband live. We will be close to the mountains. A whole new life for me after all these trials."

"How is this relationship different?"

"It's much more spiritual. Richard is my spiritual partner as well as my love. We are helping each other. I would like to say that you don't have to put your life on hold until you are finished with forgiveness. Forgiveness is an ongoing process.

"I am going through the stages of grief. I am going through the stages of forgiveness. But since Richard and I met again and fell in love, I feel that there IS another chance for love and healing and wholeness and happiness for both of us. My children adore him. My family and friends rejoice in our happiness. We have both been given another chance at whole-hearted living. And we mean to take it!"

SOULWORK, FORGIVENESS AND TRUE LOVE

"When change is accepted—no, more than that, embraced—it catalyzes our lives, expands our understanding, and shifts our perspective from one of fear to one that affirms life. For life is change."

GLORIA D. KARPINSKI

Richard is a dear friend, soft-spoken, articulate, kind. He has worked as a psychologist in the field of death and dying and with families in crisis for about twenty years. He wanted to talk of the changes that had taken place in his own life in the past year that had led to his relationship with Judy and the new life that they are about to share.

"I believe that the turning point for me in terms of forgiveness came through the necessity to take stock of my own life after I too, had experienced a traumatic loss. You remember when I met you, that ten days earlier, my very young wife, after less than five months of marriage, walked out on me without a word. I was struggling to make sense of this and to deal with my emotions of betrayal, anger and loss, when we had our first talks.

"Here I was, a respected psychologist in the field of grief and loss, working with families in crisis, working with the hospital and hospice care and death and dying groups. And I couldn't even handle my own life! And I didn't feel like there was anyone I could turn to, although now, looking back, I see that my friends did help—they were there for me.

"But at the time I remember thinking that somehow it was all my fault. I had screwed up yet again and that somehow God knew, God was laughing at me, God was punishing me. I kept thinking that all I wanted was to give and receive love, and yet here was my second marriage on the rocks without even a clue from the other person involved.

"We had a lot of talks, I remember, and I poured myself into my work—What else is new?—but it wasn't until I did a whole year of intense, introspective inner soulwork with myself, that my life began to change.

"You asked me about my steps toward forgiveness. Yes, I wrestled with forgiveness daily for I don't know how long, and I thought I had forgiven my ex-wife, and all the other women I had ever been involved with over the years. I thought I had recognized my patterns and taken prayerful steps not to repeat them.

"Then one day, it was right after I had met Judy again and was telling you of the sweetness and the gift that this lovely woman represented in my life, and yet not really believing that I could at last find happiness with any woman, that you said something to me that was so important I have never forgotten it. You said, and I'm quoting here because I wrote it down, 'Richard, you'll never be able to heal your chaotic relationships with women until you give up your grudge against God.'

"This was really profound. No one had ever told me

that before in all my years of counseling and being counseled. Part of my ongoing soulwork has consisted in getting out of my head, out of analyzing everything and everyone and instead just going into my spiritual quest. And when I realized that I did indeed have a grudge against God, an ancient and ongoing grudge that had gone on for many years, I decided to start there. By forgiving God. And by forgiving the universe for, or so it seemed to me at the time, withholding my good from me, denying me, punishing me, playing games with me, you name it. Forgiving the universe and God for not supplying me with all I wanted.

"I felt entitled. Look at all that I had done for others! Then I realized that I was not entitled any more than anyone else or any less than anyone else. Yet I wanted proof of my entitlement. A visible sign from God. Look at all I had given to other people and their projects, dreams, hopes, wishes. Look at how I had helped those in grief and need. I had done it all out of a full heart and a desire to help others. And yet. 'It's supposed to come back to me,' or so I argued within myself. It was a continual inner conflict, a continual inner dialogue—griping at God, hating myself.

"Then I would often find myself denying or walking away from or turning my good down. I thought I did it out of love. I was both pushing against and pulling for my own good at the same time. I was an internal gyroscope. One day North, one day South. Mixed directions and mixed messages.

"What changed?"

"Seeking the kingdom within. Looking at my self and my patterns with rigorous honesty. That's when I realized that I required forgiveness of my self. Of all past failures and past relationships. I was afraid of what I'd find. So I blamed God and circumstances instead. I was afraid that I would find that indeed I did not do all this on my own— that Someone WAS there in both the good and the bad times. That's when my spiritual quest and spiritual growth really began.

"You asked me when we first met what I was looking for in my life. I answered 'Soulwork.'

"'That's interesting,' you said. 'I just finished writing a book on the subject.' Well the hairs just rose on my neck. And so we became good friends. And now one year later, I have a new life, a new beginning, and the woman of my dreams. How disastrous it would have been if I had stayed in that old mismatched relationship! I wish the past and the people in it the very best. I forgave and it gave me back my life.

"Yet forgiveness is never finished. It's a process of finding your way home. Home to yourself. Home to God. Home to your own true wholeness. It's a sustaining process, as well as a searching process."

"What made you take a leap into a new life and a new love with Judy? What made you take such a risk?"

"The answer came to me from within. Faith is required to trust and go forward even through all the unknowing.

161

'You gotta do it to get it.'

"I want more and more faith. I keep asking for it. 'Faith grows stronger by exercise,' as you once told me. Yet I feel an apprehension even as I say that statement. I want to be stronger spiritually, but does this mean that I have to lift more weight? I know that I have to stretch more. I know that I am a limitless individual. There are limitless possibilities for me. I want to live consciously. I want to find as much of me as I can find. There are parts of me that are not lost, just unexplored. This takes a giant leap of courage. The future may not be better, but at least you do it. I have a lot to lose but more faith to just do it. It's exciting and inspiring. This in itself creates more faith. It's a positive cycle.

"Ten years ago, I thought that I could project forward into the same future or throw myself into an abyss. The not-knowing was excruciating. Now, I project forward and trust that my greatest good will appear.

"As you grow in faith, you have more to give your clients, more for them to connect with. I remember a quotation attributed to Mark Twain—about thinking when he was fourteen that his father was a fool, yet when he became a man at twenty-one, he saw that his father was wise. This has happened to me.

"I am deeper now, so my clients can be deeper in their work with me. I remember one client, Cathy. She is now learning to be happy in herself. Her animosity and blame is almost gone. She forgave her husband and self and all those ego projections that blamed others for her own unhappiness. Twenty years ago, even ten years ago, I wouldn't have had as much to give her in therapy. Now I see my work as a continuing quest. I am not here to alleviate symptoms. One client told me that coming to therapy for her now is like coming home. This client is the wife of the man I held in my arms as he died and told him that he was a winner, that he had changed the world by his presence. This client started seeing me for stress-related problems. Our first session lasted over three hours. I can't cut people off at a 50-minute hour. Her original goal was to learn to meditate to alleviate her stress. Now she is coming back to God.

"When I meet with people now, I have no agenda. I let them lead. It's their life. It's their story. It's their healing. As a therapist, I feel that it's not traditional therapy that works—it's the spirituality when two people meet to resolve their life issues. There needs to be a marriage of psychotherapy and spirituality. I try to be available to that union.

"Everyone needs unconditional love and acceptance. That's what I give in these sessions. That's what I try to give in my own life. You want to provide a space for love to come in. The more I have, the more I have to give. It also works in receiving. My own life is evidence of that. I can extrapolate these truths I am being taught to friendships and to my own personal relationship with Judy.

"If you had told me even a year ago that this was in store for me, I would have laughed and thought that you were crazy. Now I am moving to Colorado with the love of my life. We will live in a small town in the mountains, near her daughter and husband. We're both starting over. New place, new livelihood, new relationship. I used to long for crisp, cool air and snow-topped mountain peaks. I used to long for simplicity. All that I have ever longed for is coming true at last. But first I had to learn to forgive the past. And to give up my grudge against God."

"We must develop and maintain the capacity to forgive. He who is devoid of the power to forgive is devoid of the power to love. There is some good in the worst of us and some evil in the best of us. When we discover this, we are less prone to hate our enemies."

MARTIN LUTHER KING, JR.

CHAPTER FOURTEEN

••••

Forgiveness In The Workplace

"**W**ell," I would imagine you are wondering, "Who are YOU to tell me that I should forgive my nasty boss, my exasperating co-workers, my employees? Who are you to tell ME that I should spread the wings of forgiveness over the people I like and the people I don't like, the people I trust and the ones I am wary of? Who are you to tell me that I should forgive mismanagement, unfairness, incompetence, etc., etc., etc.?

No one IS telling you anything about shoulds or musts. But. Once you start the forgiveness process and incorporate it into your life, it will, without a doubt, spill over into other areas of your life.

Sometimes people confuse forgiveness with approval. Sometimes they confuse forgiveness with passivity. Seldom do we realize, until and unless we have been practicing the steps of forgiveness for a very long time, that forgiveness is about discernment and wisdom and tolerance, and yes, dare I say it?—forgiveness is ultimately about mastery.

There is a certain sort of balance that comes into play within when we are able to gradually but definitely let go of our fighting stance against the world. We are so quick to rush to anger, to judge, to criticize, to condemn.

A friend of mine who is having a difficult time with judgment and tolerance discovered to her amazement that she was constantly and unremittingly judging herself. She was, of course, constantly judging others as well. This was no trivial response. This was Kamikaze action, a psychic gun shooting at her constantly and bringing down everyone in her path as well.

"I would start a new job, or start a new course of study," she explained, "and then I would unrealistically set myself up to fail. I would unrealistically expect others to meet my needs. Then I would condemn them when they fell off the pedestal I had set them upon. I was constantly disappointed in my interactions with other people. Pretty soon I concluded that all bosses were unfeeling, all co-workers unkind, all peers untrustworthy. Only when I finally looked within myself, for a very long and continuing time of reflection and evaluation, did I conclude that I was always judging myself, and finding myself unfeeling and unkind, nasty, unworthy, incompetent, untrustworthy, and of course, thoroughly and completely unlovable and unredeemable. I did a lot of painful soul-searching. I determined to change my patterns of reacting to the world. It's amazing how your judgments of other people begin to change when you have stopped judging yourself. My life is far from being all sweetness and light, but at least I don't automatically make everyone else my enemy."

She is a young woman in her thirties, and has worked since she was sixteen. She is just now beginning to feel that she is in charge of her career path. But she has made an important shift in her consciousness. She has decided to look first within herself before she blames others. Most of us have enough maturity to do this some of the time. But it is easier, in our culture, to blame and separate, to set up victims and villains, than it is to navigate through life with as much balance and kindness as we can muster.

There is another component to forgiveness of that vast majority of other people out there. That quality is one of discernment. The older I grow, the less I choose to waste my energies on people and activities that lead me into a confused tangle of energies and agendas. I constantly ask for clarity and discernment in a work situation. I have been a president of a small company. I have been an employee. I have been a teacher. I have been a student. I have been self-employed now for a number of years. I made some mistakes along the way, in whatever hierarchy I was in at the time.

Finally I decided that for me, self-employment was best because it allowed me more autonomy and freedom. It allowed me more mastery over my time and who or what I allowed into my space. I still deal with contracts and agreements, I still deal with deadlines and pressures, both those of money and of time, I still have to produce work that is contracted for and then judged by those who pay me for my words. But I am no longer fighting the world. Along the way to forgiving myself, others, God, etc., the forgiveness spilled over into areas of my work.

Oh I occasionally get riled and frustrated at injustice, incompetence, stupidity, and office politics. But I can't change any of these tangles. I can only change my reaction to them. If forgiveness is a vital step toward mastery, then I will forgive and forgive and forgive again until like the old prayer, I will know to change the things I can change, to let go of the things I cannot change, and have the wisdom to know the difference. I'm still learning this, so apply what you will to your own situation.

A dear friend of mine, who in her long, steady, satisfying, commonsensical life, had felt little need or reason to forgive, was faced with a number of challenges soon after she retired from the school system. Her mother-in-law's Alzheimer's disease had worsened, her mother was debilitated by a stroke, a broken hip, and heart disease, and her beloved husband, after many years of running his own construction company, (with the addition of a silent, retired partner the last few years), was diagnosed with lung cancer and given three months to live.

Throughout all this, my friend, with remarkable courage, took charge and supported her family in heroic fashion. Her husband put all his affairs in order, managing to provide for his wife, his son, his mother, and her mother. He wanted to keep his company open for business, but he owed his retired partner $100,000. He hung on to life until he felt that his estate would cover that debt as well.

The one thing he asked of his wife was not to tell his partner of his illness. In fact, she shielded him from well-meaning friends and colleagues for months, as he valiantly strove to continue his work until the last minute. Whether she agreed with his decision or not I do not know, but she respected his wishes. When her husband died, she kept his company running without one day of closure. It was their livelihood. It was her link to her husband's dream.

But her resolve faltered when it came to her husband's partner. One day she called me long-distance. The most stoic woman I knew was crying so hard I could barely understand what had happened. "Today I had to meet with my lawyer and my husband's partner," she said, "And turn over to him, just two weeks after my husband's death, the $100,000 owed to him. I have never had any reason or need to forgive," she continued, "but I needed forgiveness today. Why couldn't he have waited until we were sure that the company my husband spent a lifetime building up would survive? Why couldn't he have come to me and expressed his friendship by allowing us six months to a year, or even forgiving the debt? I have two ill old women to care for, as well as providing for my son and myself. I have a company of loyal employees that need to be paid. It was one of the hardest things I've ever done," she went on, "to stand in that office and turn over that check to my husband's partner. And he didn't make it any easier. He couldn't even look me in the eye. I got through the meeting without breaking down. But I have cried all the way home. This is a hard one for me to forgive. But I will do it."

Much later, my friend and I talked about this difficult time in her life, and of her anger and hurt at her husband's partner. "There was something I didn't realize at the time," she told me. "I was in a state of shock and grief, and doing the very best I could, under the devastating circumstances. It was one of the few times in my life when I failed to take into consideration the other person's point of view.

"My husband's partner was grieving too. He was heartbroken that my husband refused to let him into his life during the last months of his illness. He was bereft that he had not known of the severity of the illness, and had not been able to say good-bye to his partner and his friend. He wanted his name taken off the company offices. He wanted some changes that seemed petty to me. He wanted his money. He wanted everything he thought was owed to him in the midst of this tragic situation. It took me some time before I could understand the extent of his grief. He had lost a partner and a friend.

"Once I understood, we were able to come together as friends and forgive each other for the hard thoughts we had held during this time of crisis. It was a swift but terrible lesson in forgiveness for me. I had always been able to put myself in the other person's shoes and understand their point of view.

"Now that I have forgiven the situation, I am able to do so again. So if you need a story of forgiveness in the workplace, you can tell your readers this one."

APPLYING THE SEVEN STEPS
OF FORGIVENESS IN THE WORKPLACE

"There's an exciting journey ahead and each of us has the opportunity to create our own path. The future is going to come within each of us based on who we uniquely are, rather than from forces operating outside of us."

WILLIAM BRIDGES

Many of us do not have companies to run. We feel instead, that we are run by others. We may long for more autonomy, more creativity in our own workplace. We may long to start our own businesses, explore another course of study, rearrange our lives so that we are not so stress-oriented.

If this longing for change resonates within you, why not apply the seven steps of forgiveness to the work situation as well as to the other situations in your life? It won't hurt. It can only help. And maybe just maybe, things will change.

Someone once told me—it was in a long-ago spiritual class—that when we make a decision to change within a situation with another person, one of three things happens. The person or situation changes, the other person changes or leaves, or we change or leave. I have found this to be true. It's back to that old example of energy again. When we make a decision to change, the energy changes in the situation, it affects the other person, it affects us, and then something happens to change the situation and the people involved. I use this analogy often when I seemingly hit a stone wall in negotiations, deadlines, unrealistic expectations (I know that one well!), or any other aspect of my work life. This may seem far afield from forgiveness, but it is a part of it. It is a part of the energy of forgiveness. It is a part of discernment, wisdom, and balance. And it works. It works for me. Maybe it will work for you too.

I believe that as you apply the seven steps of forgiveness to your own unique situation in the workplace, your work and your workplace will change. As you grow more peaceful, as you grow more tolerant, as you grow wiser, your energies may not track with an aggressive cutthroat corporation or a bureaucratic atmosphere. You may very well find a need to change your work and your workplace as you change. Be willing to let go of old work arenas, old areas of conflict. You will be led into your right place.

Here is what Emerson had to say about trust and the workplace. "Trust thyself: every heart vibrates to that iron string. Accept the place that divine providence has found for you, the society of your contemporaries, the connection of events."

And that is one of the gifts of change and healing. That

as we grow more harmonious and peaceful within, we are led into a more harmonious environment as well. We connect with the events, the people, the situations that are designed for our highest good.

You are going for a more peaceful, balanced, wise and loving life. So of course your circumstances will change. It's a wise lesson in trusting the universe and trusting yourself. See where you will serve best and be happiest. Then walk into your destiny without fear.

"Fear is False Evidence
Appearing Real."

UNKNOWN

CHAPTER FIFTEEN

••••

Forgiveness And Fear

Valerie is a beautiful, slender, dark-haired young woman who is both artistically talented (she is a children's book author and artist), and a single parent with a young son. For years she has struggled to find a way to support her creative work, as well as to support herself and her son. She talked to me about her ongoing search for financial and creative stability, as well as her search for love.

"I've never equated fear and forgiveness before. Or lack of fear coupled with lots of forgiveness, I should say. I really never thought about forgiveness at all. There was just too much fear. I just know that there is a way for me to break these childhood and adult messages of lack and fear. It is a genetic heritage. It took me a long time to see that. It's taking me longer to work through it. I cannot begin to tell you what the fear feels like. It used to be overpowering. Now, as I own my own power, as I face the fear, it becomes more manageable. But I need a lot more help, a lot more clarity, a lot more practice in order to overcome it. The fear is like these dark, clinging strands that come to me from out of the past, that enfold me and attach themselves to me. It's like a web of dark, malignant thoughtforms. I'm expressing, in my artwork, the cutting and the dissolving of these strands of lack and limitation, this web of fear."

I asked Valerie if I could ask her some questions about forgiveness that would help her in telling her story. She agreed and we went through the basic forgiveness questions that I have used for other interviews. Each time I use these questions, I am amazed at the stories that come forth from each individual. Valerie's story was unique in that it was as much about her creativity as about her fear, more about how far she had come in mastering her fear as well as the current challenges she faced.

"Who is the person or situation you have most needed to forgive over the years?"

"My mother, most definitely. It seems to me that all of my fears about lack of money, about lack of ability, about lack of being able to make it in the world came from her. She was a frustrated actress that never made it. She projected onto me all of her frustrations. She wanted me to be what she could never be. Yet she ringed me around with fear that of course it wouldn't happen. Part of my own empowerment has been in speaking out against that emotional abuse. Not blaming. Just getting clear. Determining not to follow that family pattern, that family web."

"Tell me the story of what happened that necessitated forgiveness on your part."

"Well there are several stories. One is about my childhood. One is about my marriage and my young son and my

177

divorce. One is about my search for love and creativity. One is my search to support myself and my eleven-year-old-son Brian. I won't go into details of what happened in my marriage. It was abusive, both to me and to my son. I left my husband because of my love for my son. I don't want him to be an unempowered man. I stood my ground and continue to stand my ground on abusive situations. I will and do speak out now, whether it is a situation at the private school my son attends, or a situation with his father, or a work situation. I now go beyond my old, accustomed ways to take care of my son. When difficulties loom, where once my teeth would chatter in fear and I would be paralyzed, now I stand my ground and speak up. It's part of my own healing. It's part of healing the fear. Situations still come up, but now when things come around, I move through the fear quicker."

"What steps did you take to forgive the various persons or situations?"

"Well I do stand my ground, as I've said. And that's the hardest thing for me to do. But I still beat up upon myself. Now I'm learning, though, to own my own boundaries. To set boundaries and not let everyone walk all over me. I don't know if that's forgiveness. I don't know if I've even gotten to forgiveness of some old lifelong patterns yet, but I do know that I have changed. I am dealing with the fear. I am cutting the dark strands of the past that held me afraid and immobile. It used to be that I felt my mother as a very invasive person. She couldn't or didn't recognize boundaries. It felt like she took me over. To make me into the person she wanted to be.

"But I'm a grown-up. I have a child to take care of. I must take care of myself. So I am very aware of boundaries now. Remembering what they are. Remembering who I am. And working through the fear. Here's an example.

"Recently there was an incident at the private school my son attends. He is a scholarship student, and so I have hesitated to make waves, even though I had two occasions to witness one of the teachers out of control and behaving in an inappropriate manner. Finally I decided to speak up. Another mother and I went to the principal. We asked for changes to be made. At first he treated both of us in a condescending manner. We persisted, and over the course of several meetings with several different people at the school, we managed to make our voices heard and our position clear. We are still working on this situation. I don't know how it will be resolved in the long run. But I have taken a stand for my son's well-being. I have spoken out and I will continue to do so until some much-needed changes are made. All the while I was shaking in my shoes, but I faced my fear. Just as I faced my fear when I left my husband. Just as I faced my fear when my child needed me to act for him in another family situation regarding my ex-husband. I guess that I am getting lots of practice in facing my fears."

"So you are still actively engaged in forgiving both the past and present situations?"

"Yes. I'm right in the middle of it all. This would be a different story if I had resolved this major issue of fear and forgiveness. I am still struggling to find my boundaries. Not to let people walk all over me. I am still defending a shaky sense of self. Forgiving my self is crucial to resolution of this terror. Every situation I encounter is like a mirror image to me. When I continue to beat up on myself and find myself afraid and another situation comes up in front of my face for me to look at, it's like looking right into a mirror.

"And I am doing more than setting boundaries. I am using my art to help heal myself. One of the things I am doing is drawing pictures of childhood situations and current situations and how they appear to me. I put in everything, even the dark webs and the dark strands that enfolded me in the past. But now, after a lot of counseling and a lot of inner work, I am changing the pictures. In my new pictures I have devised a set of balloons of strength and positive intent that come into the space where the fear is. I started out by calling them bombs. The bombs were deflecting the fear. But I am not willfully or maliciously bombing the people and the situations in my life. I refuse to add to the darkness. Instead, I am using the brightly colored balloons to deflect and dissolve the old fears. This is a very powerful technique for me. My pictures are changing as I am changing."

"What have you learned as a result of this work with forgiveness and fear?"

"I realize that in the past, I thought of myself as a complete failure. There was no hope for me. But now I ask myself what would it take to give up seeing myself as a failure? What would it take for me to see myself as a success? What would it take to move out of the old ways of living in chaos, with chaotic emotions? When I don't forgive myself, then the situation continues. How am I going to respond? I ask myself, with fear or faith? So now I want to learn how to take orderly steps—not chaotic ones—to get out of the maze of my old thinking. And the more I forgive the past and forgive the fear—I always come back to that!—the more peaceful and creative and balanced I can be."

"What advice would you like to give others concerning forgiveness?"

"I have found that I don't have to throw out everything in my past, everything I thought I was, in order to get rid of the fear. I'd like to keep my vulnerability, my creativity, my sense of sensitivity. This is how I respond to the world as a gentle woman. So vulnerability, creativity, and sensitivity are not bad. They don't trip me up as I once thought. But you can be vulnerable and not let other people walk all over you. I am not a victim. I used to be. I used to feel like a mushy noodle inside. Now I have an inner contract with myself. I tell myself that I am a loving and gentle and creative woman. It's OK for me to be who I am. I can be strong as well as vulnerable. I believe that we have to have these inner contracts with ourselves. And we have to give ourselves permission to change the inner contracts that are no longer working. Only we can do this.

"You have to break the old belief systems You change the words you say to yourself in order to forgive the self. You tell yourself, 'I am not a bad child. I am a scared child.' You tell yourself that 'I am not a victimized woman, I am a victorious woman.' You keep on changing your inner relationship to yourself. And you keep on facing the fear and forgiving the fear and forgiving the people in the past who instilled the fear in you. And you get better. I often use color in my drawings to symbolize where I am. I draw pictures of what I am trying to change. These can be before pictures and after pictures. These drawings are part of my journey away from fear and toward forgiveness. I have written a set of children's books that deal with values. One is on honesty. As I am honest with myself, then I can pass on what I have learned. But more than that, I can provide, in my children's books and my drawings, a different way for children to learn. A more positive, brave, gentle, joyful way for children to learn.

"Once I felt that the power of love was just a myth, just for other people. I felt I had never known the power of love or if I had, somewhere or somehow I had forgotten the power of love. But as the love within me gets brighter and the dark fear subsides, then I realize that there really are only two ways that you can live in the world. There is the power of fear. And there is the power of love. And I choose love. For myself. For my son. For our future. And forgiveness melts away the fear."

"All of us have the potential to be creative. Of course, we don't always develop and express our creativity but the capacity is there.
We just need to be willing to take risks, to go beyond the ego. People who are expressing their creativity do share one important trait.
They are able to act in spite of their imperfection."

AMIT GOSWAMI

CHAPTER SIXTEEN

····

Forgiveness And Creativity

Lynda Poston-Smith is a both a professional classical singer and has been a professor of voice at various universities and in private classes for over twenty years. She equates her singing with her soul. I interviewed her in a sunny peaceful garden at her home, right after she had completed a class, and as she prepared to launch her music CD, "Steal Away Home," which contains messages of hope and healing for those in hospice care and for those who work with the dying. We talked about creativity and forgiveness from her unique perspective.

We began by talking about judgment.

"Judgment is a death knell to creativity, especially to a singer. The best singing comes with a sense of freedom. Even the freedom to make ugly sounds—to play with the sounds, to explore and experiment on your way to becoming a singer. There is a difference between judgment versus discernment. Inside yourself is the ultimate judge of creativity. Singers, as well as all creative people, need to forgive the self for not measuring up to our own standards. We need playfulness. The more we have, the less judgment we bring into the area of creativity. Then the less forgiveness is needed. There is no need to separate forgiveness from other activities.

"A wise teacher once told me that what we think of in our culture as 'sin' is merely imbalance. It is the separation from self and God. I believe that forgiveness is a part of reconciliation, bringing us back to wholeness, bringing us back to center. We are always striving for this wholeness and centering.

"Perfectionism doesn't work in creativity. Life mirrors art. Singing mirrors life. I can tell who my students are by the way they sing. Most of them are afraid of risk. They are tuned into perfectionism. They feel that they are never going to do something until it's perfect. Consequently, they won't risk, won't jump into adventure. They box themselves in.

"I myself am a recovering perfectionist. My own father and mother, unfortunately, never recovered from their own perfectionism, which of course they taught me. They taught me well. I was told that there were three ways of being in the world. 'The right way, the wrong way, and Mother's way.' There was no freedom to play, to try, to explore. There is no freedom in perfectionism.

"Now I see creativity as a circle, a circle of play, adventure, forgiveness, nonjudgment."

"This reminds me of *Zen and the Art of Writing* by Ray Bradbury, wherein he says that we create, essentially, by not thinking, not judging, just being in the flow."

"Yes. The older I get, the more I try to be playful in my

teaching methods. The educational system distresses me. When we are told or we teach that there is only one 'right way,' and that way alone should be followed, we lose the sense of exploring and discovery. Sometimes the easiest way is the best way.

"I feel like there is a chain around people who say, 'It's got to be right or not at all,' especially in regard to performance. They are always apologizing for their performances, whether in class or in front of an audience.

"The very first thing I ask my students is this: 'Tell me what's good about your singing if you had to describe it to a Martian.' The students are dumbfounded. 'What do you mean?' Everyone knows what's wrong with their voice, but almost no one knows what's right with their voice. So I ask my students, 'Give me a litany of what is good about your voice.' Invariably I get a list of self-criticisms. They are always seeking forgiveness for what is wrong with them and with their voices. Change and growth are more difficult when you focus on what's wrong. Change and growth are easier when you focus on what is good about what you are and in this context, what you are with your voice. This is what I tell them. Then my students can come to a realization that art, in this case, their voice, their instrument, is like life after all. They come to a realization that they are a work in progress. It's like cutting away a mountain and seeing layers."

I shared with Lynda my idea that creativity is more of a

187

getting to the heart of things, rather than adding layers on from the outside. "There's a different configuration when you look at life that way. It's like slicing away layers like the rings on a redwood tree. And we are the redwood tree, with so much strength and sturdiness. We are more a force of nature than a rigid box of ideas."

"So we learn to carve away layers of fear, guilt and shame. Our instrument is our psyche. With the voice, there is no way you can see what you're doing. Not like in painting, sculpting, writing. The mechanism is controlled through imagery. What we reveal through the voice is vulnerability, a sense of being naked and exposed before the audience. It is both physiological and psychological. There is nothing between you and your audience.

"Here's another difference. If I judge you as a pianist, I judge your playing. If I judge you as a singer, well, my voice is ME. It's very personal. It's an affront when we are judged by ourselves and others. When someone says for example, 'I like your voice, but not your singing,' I think to myself, 'Oh no! I AM my voice. My voice is me. I am my singing. My singing is me.'

"Here is the gift, the teaching if you will, that I give my students. I ask them to pull the gift of who they are out of the body. BE the instrument. Don't judge.

"I can tell when my students have difficulty in singing. When they can't or won't sing. It's like a soul sickness. If you are singing from the heart, if you are singing heart music, you can tell if someone is sick within their soul. Because in singing, the instrument is encased in one's musculature. When the body is used as an instrument, when you are physically stiff, it shows in your singing. So emotion, from anxiety to depression to anger, really affects singing. When it is hard to speak, it is hard to sing. The throat closes up. Then you have to do whatever is necessary to clear the instrument, to heal the instrument. This process or procedure or necessity for clearing and change is not a liability. It's an asset. Because once you have worked through this, the closing of the throat, the closing up of emotions, once you have opened to your power in the throat rather than hiding and closing it up and forcing the emotions down, then creativity can soar to different heights."

"Actors draw upon their pain. Writers draw upon their pain. Do singers?" I asked her.

"Yes. There are different aspects to the self, different dimensions. We are, as I have heard you say, physical, mental, emotional and spiritual beings. In performance, we balance between these four aspects of our being. We start with the three, body, mind, emotions. But there is an access into the spiritual after balance comes in the mental, emotional and physical. Then the spirit flows through. Raw power flows through.

"Imbalance always demands forgiveness. Of course we are always in this balancing and forgiving process There is a difference between evaluation and judgments. Taking stock, monitoring our balance. Here is an example. If you are a pilot flying a plane, you operate out of trained discernment, to keep the vehicle flying, with constant and minute adjustments as to balance, speed, etc. When we are immersed in judgment, however, we are not operating out of either discernment or evaluation. Judgment implies comparison with others, more than or better than. Judgment implies comparison with ourselves, the gap between past performance and where we could be. In creativity, judgment like that is like a kiss of death. That's why critics are so demoralizing to a singer, in fact to anyone engaged in a truly creative path. It's hard for me to forgive or even tolerate critics! They take the playfulness out of the arts.

"For the students, there is a path in front of them and a path behind them. I tell them not to look at someone else's path. Look at your own capacity. Look at your own measure. Look at your own potential. Don't look sideways at someone else's path.

"Sometimes I feel like I am more a spiritual counselor or a creativity counselor than a singing teacher. There's a reason why there's a box of tiissues on my piano. Sometimes it's used more than the keys. When my students are distraught and judgmental and exhausted with their own struggles, I ask them, 'Don't you think God loves you just for BEING? Not just for DOING?' I also share this with my friend who is an orchestra conductor. She told me once that one reason she stays up at night is 'that if I haven't accomplished everything, I can't go to bed. I can't relax until and unless everything is done. I've got to get everything done!'

"So I often remind her that she is worthwhile just by being who she is. She has to forgive herself for NOT doing everything, now, at once, perfectly."

"This is an area I am still working on," I told her. "Sometimes I confuse discipline and momentum, two valuable and constant tools I use to write my books, with the process of creativity itself. Then I begin to measure and to judge and the flow of creativity is muted. Then I'm working by sheer willpower, instead of harnessing my willpower to the flow of spirit. And the same can be said for our forgiveness process. We learn a way that works for us, we practice, we see the results by the changes in our own lives. But we can't control the way it happens. We can do the work, but we can't control the outcome, even in forgiveness work. Especially in creative work. And more and more I begin to see that they are the same."

"How can you quantify inner work? How do we decide where forgiveness comes in? How arrogant to think that forgiveness comes in only a certain way or at a certain time or with extreme and constant effort. Maybe God was working through you today. But it's not only what we do at various stages of our lives but how we judge ourselves and our lives. Remember when you were a teenager? Everything was black and white, no shades of gray. The lines were sharply delineated. There was a struggle and a testing of boundaries, both your own and of those adults around you. Yet adulthood is shades of gray. More than that, adulthood, I believe, is every color, every shade, every nuance. I believe that there is more than one way to sing, get to heaven, work, create. If you are stuck in rigidity, in one right way, then there is lots of time spent in judging and then forgiving. Can we, instead, as creative souls, feel free to experiment and explore, find the way that is true for us?

"If you are attuned to your body, emotions, mind, and soul, you know what is true. It resonates within you, like a tone. The acoustical definition of resonance is reinforcement. Resonance reinforces the sound. We can apply this principle to spiritual reinforcement. Then we are in tune. Yet the necessity of being in tune presupposes change. If I am in tune with my body, I may have to change as my body becomes older or feels different. I change. My body changes. My states of energy change. We can apply this to spirit. What seems true today may be different tomorrow.

"When we apply these principles of tone and resonance to the truth about ourselves, striking our true tone, being our true self, then we come around again to all that we were talking about earlier about letting go of judgment and perfectionism so that we can experience an acceptance of self. Isn't that what true forgiveness is? The acceptance of our own true self, right where we are now, learning, creating, experiencing, exploring? This is what I tell my students. This is what I want to tell your readers. Forgiveness IS creativity, as much as it is anything else. So it all, in a never-ending cycle of letting go and creating and changing, ultimately and irrevocably comes back to forgiveness."

Courage is the price that life exacts
for granting peace."

AMELIA EARHART

CHAPTER SEVENTEEN

····

The Ultimate Forgiveness Of Self

Forgiveness takes practice. Forgiveness takes courage. One wise meditator tells us that in order to grow, we have to give up our hatred. While anger can often be an energetic fuel that moves us forward into change and growth, anger, in and of itself, works only as a temporary tool. Behind the anger, if there is hatred, it must burn itself out and be released eventually, through prayer and meditation, in a deep and private process that is individual for each of us. It is a choice we make, or else we remain stuck forever at a place that feels more like Hell every day.

If we believe that love, not hate, is the motivating power of the universe, then it is only one more step to believing that as we exchange love for hate within the deepest, hidden, most sacred and profound parts of our being, then our lives will indeed manifest more love than hate, more forgiveness than resentment, and more joy than we can now imagine in our present state of development.

I have had lots of practice in forgiveness. I remember especially a three-day seminar held at an Episcopal Church in Santa Monica, California, several years ago. The focus was on forgiveness and the seminar was presented by an energetic woman in her eighties who had not only written a book on forgiveness but was affiliated with an international psychological organization who worked with the unity of spirituality and psychotherapy in daily life.

I was in therapy at the time, with a man and wife who worked as a team in this field. I had gone to them originally because of the deep grief I felt over the loss of my son Michael, to AIDS. Though I wrote books, ran a publishing company, lectured internationally, in between I grieved and grieved and grieved. There seemed to me to be no way in which I could reconcile my alternating feelings of anger, fear, guilt, and sorrow with the concept of a loving God, a loving son, and a loving mother who had done everything within human power to walk through the journey of death. I had no answers to age-old questions of "Why? Why This? Why me?" Although I wrote about Michael's journey in two separate books on AIDS and Death and Dying, with excerpts published in various other books, still I could not come to resolution within my own heart.

On the third day of the seminar, after days of sharing and singing and laughing and crying and prayerful release, there was still a stone of sorrow lodged deep within my heart. During the final forgiveness exercise, I retreated to a private corner behind a stone pillar, and let the tears course down my cheeks unobserved. I realized then that for all the books and seminars and therapy, I didn't know how to forgive and I didn't know who to forgive.

"Bring into your heart and mind one instance in which you feel that you have been less than loving, one instance in which you missed the mark, one instance where you have failed to forgive yourself." The words fell softly over the music.

Yourself? I had other people to forgive. What was all this about myself? One instance in which you have failed to forgive yourself. There were so many.

But into my mind there floated a single scene, a time when my son was dying and I was sleeping in his room. A time when I was awakened by his cries, and groggy with fatigue, was less than gentle with his demands for help. This courageous, luminous, loving young man asked me for something, a drink of water, to comb his hair, to help him sit up, and I was so tired that I could not comply with grace.

And that one instance in which I had been less than loving, haunted me. I was held hostage by my own failure to be loving, held hostage now, much later in time, by my failure to forgive myself for being human. Perhaps I still had a lot of people and circumstances to forgive, now that the door to awareness was open. But could I not start with forgiving myself? Could I not acknowledge and release this memory? And so I did. Tumbling out of my heart came the memory, surrendered, released. Forgiven.

Years later, I wrote about this experience in another book. I wanted to share with the reader the awesome implications of forgiveness of self. I called the passage "There Are No Monsters Here." When I give readings around the country, it is often requested. I know why. Because it is in sharing our deepest instances of the need for forgiveness along our spiritual journey that we connect with another's heart, and with another's need to forgive. And we start by forgiving ourselves. We start with our own inner anguish.

To practice the presence of love and forgiveness in every situation, requires no sweet or passive role. It is a courageous, ongoing struggle. It changes every assumption that we have held dear. It will change our creativity, our business, our relationships, our health, and our connection to Spirit. Practicing the presence of love and forgiveness changes our perceptions and our energy. It creates powerful change for you and for me.

The practice of the presence of love, as exemplified by forgiveness, forces you to give up your long-held anger, your on-going resentments, your fears of the future, your guilt about the mistakes you have made in the past. Love and negation cannot co-exist. This practice of the presence of love and forgiveness changes the very atoms and the cells within your body. It changes the way you look at yourself, others, and the world. It strips you of your defenses and of your distrust. The roles you have hidden behind for years, the persona you present to the world, the ego images that pass for truth, all dissolve with the continual practice of the presence of love and forgiveness in your life.

I believe, and many wise writers concur, that there are, basically, two motivating, driving factors in the world. These are Love and Fear. We alone make the choice as to which of the two emotions, the two paths, we will pursue. It is a lifelong task. We choose peace of mind as our single goal, whatever the conditions in our lives at the present moment. We choose forgiveness as the way we function in the world. We choose here and now instead of being trapped by the archeological garbage of the past, or the questionable future, which may change before our astonished eyes as we let go of our rigid beliefs about the way "it's supposed to be."

Along this journey toward forgiveness, one caution exists. There are many positive, well-meaning people in the world who seethe with unexpressed anger and repressed fears and unacknowledged, unhealed resentments. This is a part of the human condition. So no one is suggesting that lasting, creative and positive change can occur only in the area of pleasantness.

Often it is only when we are forced to our knees by tragedy and pain that we are open enough to even begin to look at the dark, unhealed, forlorn, unloved portions of ourselves. Usually there is pleasantness on top, like makeup skillfully applied and then frozen into mask, or like a designer suit donned as armor so that we can meet and make our way in the world, with our costume intact. While underneath there are vast and uncharted arenas of pain we have no conception of. Always, underneath the anger and the hatred and the pain, there is an inner self that longs to be received and recognized.

This task of discovering and healing the hurt self within us can take a lifetime. No one suggests that peace and love are merely coverings to be laid upon the sorrow deep within. But as we uncover and discover and love and heal the inner self, bit by bit, layer by layer, there is room and allowance for more peace and love, genuine authenticity, essential forgiveness, to flow into our thirsty hearts. And then, and only then, there is more peace, forgiveness, ease, love, and authenticity available within us to flow outward to others. Then our lives are lived in ever-increasing joy and satisfaction and wonder.

So it's not enough to change our thinking, change our minds. We must change our hearts as well. And both the first place and the ultimate place in which to extend forgiveness is to our own self. Our whole self. And let the self experience the love we have withheld from it for far too long. Forgiveness for our essential self releases energies that can transform our lives, that can transform our relationships, our work in the world, that can even transform our relationship to our Creator.

But the first step is the choice for forgiveness. And then the very steps of forgiveness can be practiced, one by one, until our relationship to our deepest, most sacred, most profound essence is transformed.

"I said to the man who stood at the gate of the year; 'Give me a light that I may tread safely into the unknown.' And he replied 'Go out into the darkness and put your hand into the hand of God. That shall be to you better than light and safer than a known way.'"

M. LOUISE HASKINS
(Quoted by his Majesty the King in a radio broadcast during World War II in England)

CONCLUSION
••••

Forgiving The World And Reaffirming The Spirit

How do we forgive the world? We forgive the world, its tumultuous upheavals, both of nations and of nature, its politics, its cruelties, its magnificent heroism and its violent, inexplicable tragedies, just as we forgive ourselves, our families, our friends, our colleagues, our communities. We forgive the world by making a difference in it. Right where we are. We forgive the world step by step. We plant gardens, we raise our families, we strive to live decent, thoughtful lives of optimism and grace. We become the heroes of our own lives.

And we reaffirm the seven steps of forgiveness in our daily lives. Daily we reaffirm. Whatever the problem, we recognize and acknowledge it. We define a situation and make a clear and conscious decision, born of our desire, for positive change. We then go within in meditation and prayer and ask for guidance. We take both inner and outer action from the guidance we have received. We look for the lessons the situation has brought to us through increasing our understanding and awareness.

And ultimately and always and without a doubt, we accept healing and change within the lessons of life that have been presented to us. We continue the cycle of the seven steps to forgiveness. We may call upon them often to help us live lives of grace and goodness, lives of wisdom and love. More than that, we cannot do.

But when we do what we can, do what we must, and trust in God for the rest, we change the world. How do we change the world? How do we change OUR world? We change our world by our very presence in it.

When we are centered in forgiveness, we are both human and transcendent. A balanced and harmonious individual walks a fine line between living in the world and living in the spirit. Most of us live in the world, not in a monastery or on top of a mountain. Daily we are faced with myriad and instantaneous choices of responding to the people, places, and events around us. So we ask ourselves the question true seekers have asked since time began. How can we live IN the world but be not OF it?

We do it for small segments of time. Waking in the silence, moving through solitary summer walks, saying a prayer as we bless our food, bless another, bless our world. Collecting our thoughts before we go to bed. Pulling the light over us as we sleep like warm covers protecting us from the dark.

Yet our lives are lived in action. We do the work of the

world. We are doing well by doing good, as the old proverb goes. We do the best we can. We yearn toward the infinite even while we keep our feet grounded firmly on the path.

What is this journey toward forgiveness? It is the journey toward self-realization. It is the journey toward love and blessing and kindness and strength and integrity and wisdom, all the attributes we may have laid down and abandoned somewhere along the way, in our rush to get and do and prove and survive and succeed. Just as we laid down our ideas about forgiveness at the beginning of this book, so that we could allow room for new ways of seeing, new ways of heart-opening, new ways of relating, new ways of understanding. Just as along the way we also laid down our judgments, our confusion, our heavy, heavy burdens of control and rigidity. Just as we dissolved the hardness in our hearts and the anger and fear and shame in our soul. Just as we began to see the patterns of our own being, and just as we began to relate differently, more harmoniously, to the people and events around us, so we take another step and another and another. Until long before we reach the end of the journey we find that we are free and clear and whole. Find that we perceive ourselves with as much gentleness as we have learned to perceive others.

This is, of course, more than the journey of the body, more than an outward expression of forgiveness. We have moved from the outer to the inner. Beyond the visible realms to the sacred inner invisible. We are living, breathing, moving, working, playing, praying from the inside out. Oh we are not and never will be perfect people. We do not even try. Because both measurement and approval have lost their power over us.

We still ride the creative, ever-expanding waves of the mind. We still ride the ever-changing, ever-expressive ocean of our emotions. But we are changed. We are changed by our willingness and our ability and our clear seeing to forgive. We are changed at depth. We are both human and spirit. And we walk hand in hand with God. Step by prayerful step. Forgiving and forgiven.

Authors And Their Quotations

206

207

LIST OF CONTRIBUTORS

How can I even begin to thank the people whose life stories made up the bulk of this book on forgiveness? Those who allowed me to use their names and those who preferred to remain unknown, all have helped me immeasurably. There are countless books, essays, proverbs, classes, and teachings from other spiritual writers that have also helped to shape my beliefs along my own ongoing journey toward forgiveness. To all of them, and to the contributors listed below, I offer my heartfelt appreciation.

Connie Courtney

Judy Goodwin

Karen Hottel

Valerie Ingle

Sandy Denke Jones

Dr. Bea Lovejoy

Dr. Richard Nesta

Rita Robinson

Lynda Poston-Smith

Connie Stockton

Nancy Ward

Philip Ward

ABOUT THE AUTHOR

BettyClare Moffatt, M.A., is a prominent writer and public speaker in the fields of inspiration, creativity, AIDS, grief recovery and women's spirituality.

She is the author of *Soulwork: Clearing the Mind, Opening the Heart, Replenishing the Spirit; When Someone You Love Has AIDS: A Book of Hope for Family and Friends; Gifts for the Living: Conversations with Caregivers on Death and Dying, Opening to Miracles: True Stories of Blessing and Renewal*, as well as several other books.

She is a widely known lecturer and has appeared on major television and radio talk shows, including *Oprah*.

BettyClare Moffatt is available for speakng engagements. Please contact MasterMedia's Speaker's Bureau for availability and fee arrangements.

Call Tony Colao at (800) 453-2887 or fax (908) 359-1647.

MASTERMEDIA LIMITED

To order copies of *Journey Toward Forgiveness: Finding Your Way Home* ($11.95) send a check for the price of each book ordered plus $2 postage and handling for the first book, and $1 for each additional copy to:

MasterMedia Limited
17 East 89th Street
New York, NY 10128
(212) 260-5600
(800) 334-8232
(212) 546-7638 (fax)
(Please use MasterCard or VISA on phone orders)

AN INVITATION

If you found this book helpful, you may want to receive an inspirational newsletter from The Heritage Imprint, a list of inspirational books from MasterMedia, the only company to combine publishing with a full-service speakers bureau.

MasterMedia books and speakers cover today's important issues, from family values to health topics and business ethics.

For the Heritage Newsletter or a MasterMedia book catalog, write or fax to the above address or phone number.

For information and a complete list of speakers, call (800) 453-2887 or fax (908) 359-1647.

THE HERITAGE IMPRINT
OF INSPIRATIONAL BOOKS

MasterMedia launches The Heritage Imprint—books that speak of courage, integrity and bouncing back from defeat. For the millions of Americans seeking greater purpose and meaning in their lives in difficult times, here are volumes of inspiration, solace and spiritual support.

The Heritage Imprint books will be supported by MasterMedia's full-service speakers' bureau, authors' media and lecture tours, syndicated radio interviews, national and co-op advertising and publicity.

Resiliency:
How to Bounce Back Faster, Stronger, Smarter
Tessa Albert Warschaw, Ph.D. and
Dee Barlow, Ph.D).

Resiliency is packed with practical techniques and insights on solving old problems in new ways. It also shows readers how to become more resilient in their personal and professional lives and teaches the skills for bouncing back from everyday stresses to surviving disastrous multiple losses. You will learn to enthusiastically embrace life. [$21.95, *Resiliency: How to Bounce Back Faster, Stronger, Smarter*. Hardbound ISBN 1-57101-021-1, October.]

The Ethical Edge:
Tales of Organizations
That Have Faced Moral Crises
Dawn Marie Driscoll, W. Michael Hoffman, Edward S. Petry, associated with The Center for Business Ethics at Bentley College.

The authors link the current search for meaning and values in life with stories of corporate turnarounds. Now read about organizations that have recovered from moral crises—the tough lessons they've learned, ethical structures they've put in place to ensure a solid future. If every employee followed the mission of the book, America's companies would clearly have not only a moral edge, but a competitive edge. [$24.95, *The Ethical Edge: Tales of Organizations That Have Faced Moral Crises*. Hardbound ISBN 1-57101-051-3, February.]

Heritage:
The Making of an American Family
Dr. Robert B. Pamplin, Jr., with Gary Eisler, Jeff Sengstack and John Domini. Foreward by Norman Vincent Peale.

Fascinating saga of the Pamplin family, which has built one of the largest private fortunes in America. From the Crusades to today's multi-million dollar corporation run by the author and his father, longtime head of the Georgia-Pacific Corporation. [$12.95,.Heritage: *The Making of an American Family*. Paperbound ISBN 1-57101-041-6, June.]

Prelude to Surrender:
The Pamplin Family
and The Siege of Petersburg
Dr. Robert B. Pamplin, Jr., with Gary Eisler, Jeff Sengstack and John Domini.

Engaging account of how the author's ancestral home was taken over by the Confederacy for use as a hospital and as a defensive position. It is now the Pamplin Park Civil War Site.
[$10.95,.Prelude to Surrender: *The Pamplin Family and The Siege of Petersburg*. Hardbound ISBN 1-57101-049-1, September.]

American Heroes:
Their Lives, Their Values, Their Beliefs
Dr. Robert B. Pamplin, Jr., with Gary Eisler.

Courage. Integrity. Compassion—the qualities of the hero still live in American men and women today—even in a world that is filled with disillusionment. Share their stories of outstanding achievements, and discover the values that guide their lives as revealed in a pioneering coast-to-coast survey. [$18.95,.*American Heroes: Their Lives, Their Values, Their Beliefs*. Hardbound ISBN 1-57101-010-6, June.]

OTHER MASTERMEDIA BOOKS

To order additional copies of any MasterMedia book, send a check for the price of the book plus $2.00 postage and handling for the first book, $1.00 for each additional book to:

MasterMedia Limited
17 East 89th Street
New York, NY 10128
(212) 260-5600
(800) 334-8232
(212) 546-7638
(Please use Master Card or Visa on phone orders)

AGING PARENTS AND YOU: A Complete Handbook to Help You Help Your Elders Maintain a Healthy, Productive and Independent Life, by Eugenia Anderson-Ellis, is a complete guide to providing care to aging relatives. Practical advice and resources for adults who are helping their elders lead independent lives. Revised and updated. ($9.95 paper)

BALANCING ACTS! Juggling Love, Work, Family, and Recreation, by Susan Schiffer Stautberg and Marcia L. Worthing, provides strategies to achieve a balanced life by reordering priorities and setting realistic goals. ($12.95 paper)

BOUNCING BACK: How to Turn Business Crises Into Success, by Harvey Reese. Based on interviews with entrepreneurs from coast to coast, this fascinating book contains cautionary tales that unfold with gripping suspense. Reese has discovered a formula for success that should be "must reading" for every new or budding entrepreneur. ($18.95 hardbound)

BREATHING SPACE: Living and Working at a Comfortable Pace in a Sped-Up Society, by Jeff Davidson, helps readers to handle information and activity overload and gain greater control over their lives. ($10.95 paper)

CITIES OF OPPORTUNITY: Finding the Best Place to Work, Live and Prosper in the 1990's and Beyond, by Dr. John Tepper Marlin, explores the job and living options for the next decade and into the next century. This consumer guide and handbook, written by one of the world's experts on cities, selects and features forty-six American cities and metropolitan areas. ($13.95 paper, $24.95 cloth)

THE CONFIDENCE FACTOR: How Self-Esteem Can Change Your Life, by Dr. Judith Briles, is based on a nationwide survey of six thousand men and women. Briles explores why women so often feel a lack of self-confidence and have a poor opinion of themselves. She offers step-by-step advice on becoming the person you want to be. ($18.95 cloth, $9.95 paper)

THE DOLLARS AND SENSE OF DIVORCE, by Dr. Judith Briles, is the first book to combine practical tips on overcoming the legal hurdles by planning finances before, during, and after divorce. ($10.95 paper)

THE ENVIRONMENTAL GARDENER: The Solution to Pollution for Lawns and Gardens, by Laurence Sombke, focuses on what each of us can do to protect our endangered plant life. A practical sourcebook and shopping guide. ($8.95 paper)

HERITAGE: The Making of an American Family, by Dr. Robert Pamplin, Jr., traces the phenomenal history of the Pamplin family from the Crusades to an eye-opening account of how they built one of the largest private fortunes in the United States. Heritage is an inspiring paradigm for achievement based on a strong belief in God and integrity. ($24.95, hardbound; $12.95 paper)

LIFETIME EMPLOYABILITY: How to Become Indispensable, by Carole Hyatt is both a guide through the mysteries of the business universe brought down to earth and a handbook to help you evaluate your attitudes, your skills, and your goals. Through expert advice and interviews of nearly 200 men and women whose lives have changed because their jobs or goals shifted, Lifetime Employability is designed to increase your staying power in today's down-sized economy. ($12.95 paper)

THE LIVING HEART BRAND NAME SHOPPER'S GUIDE, by Michael F. DeBakey, M.D., Antonio M. Gotto, Jr., M.D., D.Phil., Lynne W. Scott, M.A., R.D./L.D., and John P. Foreyt, Ph.D., lists brand-name supermarket products that are low in fat, saturated fatty acids, and cholesterol. ($12.50 paper)

THE LOYALTY FACTOR: Building Trust in Today's Workplace, by Carol Kinsey Goman, Ph.D., offers techniques for restoring commitment and loyalty in the workplace. ($9.95 paper)